Mathieu Ossendrijver
Conceptions of Cyclicity in Babylonian and Greco-Roman Scholarship

CHRONOI
Zeit, Zeitempfinden, Zeitordnungen
Time, Time Awareness, Time Management

Edited by
Eva Cancik-Kirschbaum, Christoph Markschies and
Hermann Parzinger

on behalf of the Einstein Center Chronoi

Volume 18

Mathieu Ossendrijver

Conceptions of Cyclicity in Babylonian and Greco-Roman Scholarship

—

DE GRUYTER

ISBN 978-3-11-914204-5
e-ISBN (PDF) 978-3-11-222425-0
e-ISBN (EPUB) 978-3-11-222426-7
ISSN 2701-1453
DOI https://doi.org/10.1515/9783112224250

This work is licensed under the Creative Commons Attribution-NonCommercial-NoDerivatives 4.0 International License. For details go to https://creativecommons.org/licenses/by-nc-nd/4.0.

Library of Congress Control Number: 2025945625

Bibliographic information published by the Deutsche Nationalbibliothek
The Deutsche Nationalbibliothek lists this publication in the Deutsche Nationalbibliografie; detailed bibliographic data are available on the internet at http://dnb.dnb.de.

© 2025 with the author(s), published by Walter de Gruyter GmbH, Berlin/Boston, Genthiner Straße 13, 10785 Berlin. This book is published with open access at www.degruyterbrill.com.

www.degruyterbrill.com
Questions about General Product Safety Regulation:
productsafety@degruyterbrill.com

Acknowledgment

This study was made possible by the generosity of the Einstein Center Chronoi, which provided me with a six-month fellowship in 2019. I want to express my gratitude to Eva Cancik-Kirschbaum, Christoph Markschies, Stefanie Rabe, Eva Rosenstock, and Irene Sibbing-Plantholt for the hospitality which I enjoyed in the Chronoi villa in Berlin-Dahlem. It was a great pleasure to exchange thoughts with them and with the other Fellows, in particular Antonio Panaino, Andreas Winkler, Ilaria Bultrighini, Menahem Ben Sasson, and Sophie Remijsen. The manuscript was finished in the framework of the project "ZODIAC – Ancient Astral Science in Transformation", which is funded by the European Research Council under the Horizon 2020 framework (Advanced Grant No. 885478).

Contents

Acknowledgment —— V

1 Introduction —— 1

2 Mesopotamian scholarly conceptions of time and luni-solar cyclicity until ca. 750 BCE —— 4
2.1 The Flood, cyclicity, and history in Mesopotamian mythology —— 4
2.2 Astronomical cycles and time in the myth *When Above* (*Enūma eliš*) —— 5

3 Conceptions of cyclicity in Mesopotamian celestial divination (ca. 750–200 BCE) —— 8
3.1 Cyclicity in the astral compendium *Mul.Apin* —— 8
3.2 Cyclicity in the celestial omen series *Enūma Anu Enlil* —— 10

4 Cyclicity in Babylonian astronomical diaries and related texts (ca. 750 BCE – 75 CE) —— 14
4.1 Astronomical diaries, Goal Year methods, and the predictive turn —— 14
4.2 Goal Year methods and their conceptualization in procedure texts —— 23
4.3 Reflections on the use of cyclicity in the astronomical diaries and related texts —— 27

5 Cyclicity in Babylonian mathematical astronomy (ca. 400–50 BCE) —— 32
5.1 Developments in the knowledge and the conceptualization of astronomical cycles —— 34

6 Planetary conjunctions in Babylonian astral science —— 37
6.1 Periods for planetary conjunctions in procedure texts —— 38
6.2 Conjunctions in Babylonian astrological historiography —— 40

7 Babylonian evidence for cyclicity beyond astronomical phenomena —— 42
7.1 Non-astronomical phenomena in the astronomical diaries and related texts —— 42
7.2 Procedures for predicting market rates and weather phenomena —— 44
7.3 Evidence for intrinsic cyclicity of non-astronomical phenomena —— 50
7.4 Babylonian horoscopes —— 51
7.5 Schematic luni-solar cycles in microzodiac texts and calendar texts —— 52
7.6 Hidden agency of the planets in Late Babylonian astrology —— 55

8   Towards a new understanding of the Late Babylonian conceptions of time and cyclicity —— 60

9   Cyclicity and cycle-based conceptions of time according to Plato and Aristotle —— 64
9.1   Cyclicity and the Great Year according to Plato —— **64**
9.2   Cyclicity according to Aristotle —— **69**

10   Cycles and cyclicity in Greco-Roman astronomy —— 72
10.1 Hipparchus and Claudius Ptolemy —— **72**
10.2 The Keskintos inscription —— **73**
10.3 The Antikythera mechanism —— **75**
10.4 The *Introduction to the Phaenomena* by Geminus —— **77**
10.5 The Oxyrhynchus papyri and the Fouad Papyrus —— **77**

11   Astronomical cycles and the Great Year in Greco-Roman astrology —— 79
11.1 Horoscopy and its possible implications for the cyclicity of human fate —— **79**
11.2 The Great Year and the periodic destruction of the universe —— **82**
11.3 Planetary Time-Lords and their rulership over human fate —— **86**

12   Concluding remarks —— 88

Bibliography —— 92

Index of Names —— 101

General Index —— 102

1 Introduction

The present study explores conceptions of cyclicity and their use in Mesopotamian and Greco-Roman scholarly sources. The purpose is not to present a universal history of cyclicity and its circulation across the ancient world, but to provide snapshots into bodies of knowledge, discourse, concepts, doctrines, theories, and practices that were developed and maintained in communities of scholars. In recent decades much research has been conducted on the experience of time in different regions and communities of the ancient world.[1] The available literature covers a wide range of aspects and practices, such as calendars and their luni-solar cycles,[2] historiography,[3] the measurement of time,[4] the social construction of time, time in mythology and religion,[5] literary sources,[6] divination,[7] and medicine.[8] The investigation aims to fill a gap by exploring aspects of temporal cyclicity that have not received much attention. In particular, previous research on Mesopotamian conceptions of time has not fully engaged with the Late Babylonian astronomical and astrological evidence. It will be argued that these sources reveal fundamental changes in the Mesopotamian understanding of time and cyclicity. Some further limitations of the present study must be noted. The focus will be on temporal cyclicity as conceived by ancient scholars; more general aspects of the conceptualization of time beyond cyclicity and the experience of time and cyclicity outside scholarly circles are only occasionally addressed. This study does not engage with the notions of cyclical time and linear time which featured prominently in studies of ancient mythology, religion, and historiography from the twentieth century. Cyclical time and linear time were treated as mutually exclusive ways of conceptualizing and perceiving time and history. The former was viewed as a product of

---

1 For the Mesopotamian conception of time and its divisions see Cwik-Rosenbach 1990; Wilcke 1999; Sallaberger 2002; Robson 2004; Maul 2008; Cancik-Kirschbaum 2009; Feliu et al. 2013; Verderame 2017; Steele 2020; Emelianov 2021b; Brandes 2023; Steele 2024.
2 Sallaberger 1993; Lehoux 2007; Brack-Bernsen 2007; Britton 2007; Steele 2007; Steele 2011b; Stern 2012; Steele 2012; Cohen 2015; Koch 2016.
3 For Mesopotamia see Glassner 2004; Selz 2019.
4 For the Greco-Roman world see Miller and Symons 2020 and the literature quoted in Singer 2021, vii, footnote 1.
5 For the Greco-Roman world see Angehrn 1996; for Mesopotamia see Robson 2004; Brandes 2023.
6 For the Greco-Roman world see Wolkenhauer 2011.
7 For Mesopotamia see Koch 2013; Koch 2016; Livingstone 2013.
8 For Mesopotamia see Steele 2017; for the Greco-Roman world see the literature quoted in Singer 2021, vii, footnote 1.

mythological thinking, the latter as an expression of rational historical thinking.[9] The rich evidence for conceptions of cyclicity from other regions of the ancient world (Egypt, Levant, Persia, Anatolia, etc.) had to be excluded entirely for practical reasons.[10]

Human existence is structured by the cyclically changing conditions of day and night, seasons, and lunar phases. These obvious manifestations of cyclicity, mediated by the apparent motion of the sun, the moon, and the stars, define a framework for the perception of time and its division into days, months, and years that underlies ancient calendars. Apart from the sun, the moon, and the fixed stars, the planets also exhibit distinct cycles in their apparent motion. In the first millennium BCE, scholars across the ancient world engaged with cyclical astronomical phenomena by observing, reporting, quantifying, predicting, and explaining them, and by drawing inferences from them. The present investigation focuses on two questions that were central to Babylonian and Greco-Roman scholars. First, if conditions on earth and human existence are undeniably affected by the cycles of the sun and the moon, then what about the cycles of the planets? Do they also affect existence on earth? If yes, then what is the nature of the connections between planetary and terrrestrial phenomena? Do the planets have causal agency or do they merely signify events on earth? Secondly, many astronomical phenomena are evidently cyclical, but what about phenomena on earth, human existence, historical events, and the universe as a whole? Are they also governed by cycles? Both questions occupied scholars in Babylonia and the Greco-Roman world, but they have not attracted much attention in modern scholarship, especially the question of planetary effects on terrestrial existence. As we shall see, the answers provided by scholars are varied, but they exhibit some important points of agreement.

The premise underlying this study is that scientific knowledge is socially constructed in communities of scholars and that the practice of creating and developing such knowledge is best interpreted in terms of modeling and worldmaking, a view on knowledge production that has gained currency in the philosophy of science since the 1960s.[11] The model-based approach acknowledges that scientific

---

9 Angehrn 1996, 66–80; Assmann 2011, 193–200; Selz 2019.
10 For conceptions of time in other regions of the ancient world see, for instance, Assmann 2011; Ben-Dov and Doering 2017; von Lieven 2017; Miller and Symons 2020; Emelianov 2021a.
11 For constructivist approaches to the history of science see Golinski 1998; for the model-based approach to knowledge production see Freudenthal 1961; Magnani and Nersessian 2002; Bailer-Jones 2002; Bailer-Jones 2009. For applications of the model-based approach and the notion of worldmaking to ancient scholarship see Lehoux 2012, Rochberg 2016, 231–273; Rochberg 2018; Rochberg 2025.

practices cannot be reduced to systems of statements connected by deductive reasoning. Knowledge about the world can manifest itself in models and simulations, which are used as tools for drawing inferences about phenomena.[12] What scholars do, in this view, is reasoning based on models of idealized phenomena, which have some connection to actual phenomena.

---

[12] For the philosophy of simulation see Winsberg 1999; Winsberg 2009. For a simulation-based view on Mesopotamian computational practices see Ossendrijver 2021b.

2 Mesopotamian scholarly conceptions of time and luni-solar cyclicity until ca. 750 BCE

In order to set the stage for exploring Mesopotamian sources from the first millennium BCE, aspects of cyclicity found in several mythological compositions from the second millennium BCE are briefly discussed. In particular the *Sumerian King List*, the Flood stories, and the myth *When Above* (*Enūma eliš*) reveal aspects of Mesopotamian scholarly conceptions of time, history, and cyclicity that continued to be influential in later discourse. Many other mythological, religious, and divinatory compositions also reflect on the role of lunar and solar cycles in marking the divisions of time.[1]

2.1 The Flood, cyclicity, and history in Mesopotamian mythology

Several Sumerian and Akkadian myths, such as the *Sumerian Flood Story*, *Atraḫasīs*, and *Gilgameš* include a story about a destructive flood, which caused the land to be completely submerged.[2] The Flood was brought about by the gods in a final attempt to wipe out all humans, whose noise had become unbearable to them. The Flood is a pivotal and singular event in the Mesopotamian conception of history, which separates the antediluvian phase from the postdiluvian phase. Apart from narrative myths, numerous other texts from different periods make reference to the Flood, which testifies to its centrality in Mesopotamian cultural memory. While annual flooding was a familiar phenomenon, there is no cuneiform evidence that the Flood was considered to be a recurring phenomenon. However, the Roman scholar Seneca ascribed such a doctrine to the Babylonian priest Berossus (third century BCE), who wrote the Greek work *Babyloniaka* (Section 11.2). We learn more about history before and after the Flood in the *Sumerian King List*, a composition attested in multiple manuscripts and versions dating between the third millennium BCE and the first centuries BCE, including a Greek version

---

[1] For the Moongod see Hätinen 2021, 90–135; for time in magical practices see Livingstone 1999; for time in divinatory practices see Koch 2013; Livingstone 2013. Engagement with the cycles of the sun and the moon can be traced back to calendrical notations in proto-cuneiform documents from the late fourth millennium BCE (Brack-Bernsen 2007; Cancik-Kirschbaum 2009).

[2] For translations of Mesopotamian myths see Foster 2005; for *Enūma eliš* see Lambert 2013; for *Gilgameš* see George 2003.

preserved in the *Babyloniaka*.³ According to the *Sumerian King List*, history began when kingship descended from the heavens and was entrusted to about eight successive kings, each of which ruled in one of about five ancient cities that existed before the Flood.

The central term in the *Sumerian King List* is the Sumerian word bala, literally "turn", which corresponds to Akkadian *palû*. Throughout Mesopotamian history, bala/*palû* denotes the period during which a king rules over a territory. As pointed out by several scholars, the meaning of this term includes a notion of rotation in the sense of the alternation of reigns and dynasties.⁴ It is therefore semantically close to the concept of cycle, except that reigns do not alternate with a fixed period. However, in Late Babylonian mathematical astronomy, *palû* became a technical term for the period of a planet (see below).⁵ The reigns of the antediluvian kings are expressed in huge numbers of years. For instance, Alalgar, the second king in some versions, reigned 36,000 years in Eridu and Enmenluana, the third king, 43,200 years in Bad-tibira. There is little agreement between the numbers in different manuscripts.⁶ A common feature is that they are multiples of 3600, corresponding to the Sumerian numeral ŠAR₂, to which is sometimes added a multiple of 60, corresponding to the Sumerian numeral UŠ. In other words, they amount to pleasantly simple expressions in the Sumerian number notation. Some of the numbers are similar to or identical with values of the Great Year mentioned by Greco-Roman scholars (Section 9).

2.2 Astronomical cycles and time in the myth *When Above* (*Enūma eliš*)

The Babylonian myth *When Above* (*Enūma eliš*), which dates to the late second millennium BCE, presents a view of the division of time by cyclical phenomena that is informed by theological and political considerations. The poem relates how the Babylonian god Marduk is elevated to king of the gods and ruler of the universe after defeating Tiamat in a cosmic battle. Tablet 5 reports how Marduk creates the stars, the moon, and the sun in order to mark the divisions of time that are constitutive of the Mesopotamian luni-solar calendar:⁷

---

3 For a study of the *Sumerian King List* see Wilcke 1988. For additional manuscripts and an overview of the versions see Friberg 2007, 236–243.
4 Glassner 2000; Glassner 2001; Glassner 2004, 8–9; Brandes 2023, 22.
5 See Ossendrijver 2012, 597.
6 See Friberg 2007, 240.
7 Translation based on Lambert 2013, 99.

> He fashioned positions for the great gods,
> created stars, their images, as constellations.
> He appointed the year, marked off divisions,
> (for) the twelve months he created three stars each.
> After the day when he organized the year
> he established the position of Nēberu to assign their leash,
> so that none should transgress or be slothful. (...)
>
> He created (the Moongod) Nannar, entrusting to him the night,
> he appointed him as the jewel of the night to apportion days,
> and month by month without ceasing he elevated him with a crown,
> (saying,) "Shine over the land at the beginning of the month,
> resplendent with horns to fix the calling of days.
> On the seventh day the crown will be half size,
> on the fifteenth day, halfway through each month, stand in opposition.
> When (the Sungod) Šamaš looks at you from the horizon,
> diminish properly and grow backwards.
> On Day 29, approach the path of Šamaš!
> [. .] the 30th day, stand in conjunction and be equal to Šamaš."

The parts of this tablet that must have dealt with the creation of the Sungod Šamaš are broken. The most important division of time is assigned to the Moongod Nanna(r)/Sîn, with the Sungod given the less prominent role of marking the years. This is consistent with the subordinate position afforded to Šamaš as son of Nanna(r)/Sîn in the Mesopotamian pantheon. Several scholars have investigated the underlying conceptions of time and cyclicity.[8] The following aspects are singled out here because of their relevance for contextualizing later developments. Time and cyclicity are not presented as having an existence independent from celestial phenomena. Even the three most fundamental intervals in the human experience of time, day, month, and year, are not conceptualized as temporal entities, but indirectly and implicitly through their heavenly indicators. The creation of these indicators is the privilege of Marduk in his capacity of king of the gods and ruler of the universe. Marduk creates them by command, which reflects his royal authority and power, with the clear implication that violations are punishable. The resulting calendrical system serves to establish and maintain his control over the universe. But his agency in arranging the division of time goes beyond the creation of celestial indicators. It includes a mechanism for verifying whether the calendar is operating correctly in the form of star lists called "three stars each". They list for each month of an ideal year three stars that should rise heliacally in that

---

[8] See in particular Robson 2004, 49–55; Cancik-Kirschbaum 2009, 39–43; Verderame 2017; Brandes 2023, 30–31, 46–55, 67–74.

month, which amounts to an empirical criterium for the alignment of the calendar with the seasons.[9] The account of the origin and the role of astronomical cycles and calendars presented in *Enūma eliš* must be interpreted in the context of Babylonian kingship and its ideological and religious underpinnings. The cyclical phenomena of the moon and the sun as indicators of the divisions of time underlying the calendar were important tools of power and control for the Babylonian kings.

---

[9] For an edition and detailed investigation of Astrolabe B, the main representative of this genre, and its relation to *Enūma eliš* see Horowitz 2014.

3 Conceptions of cyclicity in Mesopotamian celestial divination (ca. 750 – 200 BCE)

In the first millennium BCE the Mesopotamian astral sciences experienced fundamental changes. Early stages of these developments can be identified in divinatory texts. They testify to a focus on the moon, the sun, and the five planets as carriers of divine signs and they contain rudimentary quantitative knowledge of planetary motion, but no explicit references to cycles and methods that could be used for predicting planetary phenomena.

3.1 Cyclicity in the astral compendium *Mul.Apin*

The astral compendium *Mul.Apin* ("Plow Star") is attested in dozens of copies from Assyria and Babylonia dating between ca. 687 BCE and the last centuries BCE. The broad temporal and geographical distribution of *Mul.Apin* is indicative of its importance for scholars across Mesopotamia. Its date of composition is a matter of debate. As argued by Hunger and Steele,[1] it was probably written at most a few centuries before 750 BCE. In later centuries scholars continued to re-interpret *Mul.Apin* and create new astronomical schemes that elaborate on various sections of *Mul.Apin*.[2] *Mul.Apin* is mainly concerned with the fixed stars, their connections to deities, elementary lunar and solar phenomena, and celestial omens. Relatively little attention is paid to the planets, which feature in several sections. In I i 1 – ii 35 the five planets are referred to as the stars that "keep changing their positions", in II i 1 – 8 they are said to "travel the path which the moon travels", and II i 38 – 43 contains instructions for observing them and presenting offerings to them. Only II i 44 – 67 contains quantitative statements about planetary phenomena, namely their first and last appearances and the intervals of visibility and invisibility between them.[3] The first part of this section (II i 44 – 59) deals with the invisibility of the planets. Both Mercury and Venus are alternately visible in the east as a morning star and in the west as an evening star. Their synodic cycles include two intervals of invisibility, which are delimited by the synodic phenomena of morning first, morning last, evening first, and evening last. By contrast, Mars, Jupiter, and Saturn experience one interval of invisibility per synodic cycle, which is de-

---

[1] Hunger and Steele 2019, 16 – 19.
[2] See Steele 2013a.
[3] Hunger and Pingree 2019, 79 – 83.

limited by the synodic phenomena of first appearance and last appearance. The following selected passages from II i 44–50 deal with the invisibility of Venus, Jupiter, and Saturn:

> Venus disappears in the east and remains (invisible) in the sky for a month, or for 1 month and 15 days, or it remains (invisible) for 2 months, and becomes visible in the west.
> Venus disappears in the west and rises in the east on the day it disappears, or it remains (invisible) for 3 days, thirdly, for 7 days, fourthly, for 14 days, and then rises.
> Jupiter disappears in the west and remains (invisible) in the sky for 20 days, or it remains (invisible) for a month, and rises and becomes visible in the east in the path of the sun.
> Saturn disappears in the west and remains (invisible) in the sky for 20 days, and becomes visible in the path of the sun.

Before discussing these passages, the corresponding statements about the intervals of visibility from the second part (II i 60–67) are presented. The following passages pertain to Jupiter, Venus, and Saturn:

> Jupiter becomes visible in the east, stands in the sky for one year, and disappears in the west.
> Venus becomes visible either in the east of in the west, stands in the sky for 9 months, and disappears.
> Saturn, also (called) the Scales, star of the sun, becomes visible in the east, stands in the sky for one year, and disappears in the west.

The quoted passages illustrate several aspects of the conceptualization of planetary cycles that are worth pointing out (Tab. 1). First, the intervals of invisibility and visibility are presented in separate units of text. That is, the intervals of invisibility are listed first for all planets and after that the intervals of visibility. The two intervals for a given planet are not added together to obtain the duration of the synodic cycle. Secondly, the numerical values of the intervals of visibility and invisibility are highly schematic round numbers, but in reality they vary continuously about a mean value.[4] For some planets, e.g. Venus, multiple alternative values are listed for each interval and it is not made clear which pairs of values should be combined in order to obtain values for the synodic cycle. Furthermore, one looks in vain for explicit references to synodic cycles in *Mul.Apin*. In summary, the authors of *Mul.Apin* formulated quantitative statements about the constitutive intervals of the synodic cycle, but not about their total duration. This is quite revealing, because they could, in principle, have done so with the data at their disposal. The conclusion is that these scholars saw no purpose in formulating and quantifying the concept of synodic cycle.

---

4 Hunger and Steele 2019, 206; Swerdlow 1998, 24–26.

Tab. 1: Intervals of invisibility and visibility of the planets Jupiter, Saturn, and Venus according to *Mul.Apin*. Adapted from Hunger and Steele 2019, 206: Table 13.

	invisibility (morning last to evening first)	visibility in the evening	invisibility (evening last to morning first)	visibility in the morning
Venus	1 month, 1 month 15 days, 2 months	9 months	0 days, 3 days, 7 days, 14 days	9 months
	invisibility (last to first appearance)	visibility (first to last appearance)		
Jupiter	20 or 30 days	1 year		
Saturn	20 days	1 year		

3.2 Cyclicity in the celestial omen series *Enūma Anu Enlil*

Other divinatory compositions from the early first millennium BCE contain similar statements about the intervals of invisibility and visibility of the planets. In Tablet 63 of the celestial omen series *Enūma Anu Enlil* predictions are inferred from the first and last appearances of Venus in the east and in the west.[5] The omens are arranged in two distinct sequences. The first sequence covers ten synodic cycles, corresponding to an interval of 16 years. Each cycle is based on the following template:

> In Month M1 Day D1 Venus disappears in the west, N1 days it remains (invisible) in the sky, and in Month M2 Day D2 Venus appears in the east: (…).
> In Month M3 Day D3 Venus disappears in the east, N2 days it remains (invisible) in the sky, and in Month M4 Day D4 Venus appears in the west: (…).

These statements are similar to those in *Mul.Apin*, but there are some differences. First and last appearances are here arranged chronologically in combined statements. Secondly, the data are arranged in an astronomically significant set of synodic cycles, because Venus phenomena repeat near the same calendar dates and celestial positions after five synodic cycles. This can be illustrated with the data provided for cycles 1, 2, and 6 (Tab. 2). In general agreement with astronomical facts, successive instances of the same phenomenon occur on different dates

---

[5] See Reiner and Pingree 1975.

after one cycle, but they repeat near the same date after five cycles.[6] Five is the smallest whole number of synodic cycles that yields a close return of Venus in terms of dates and positions. It seems likely that the sequence of omens was deliberately continued for ten cycles in order to display this repetitive aspect. This is suggestive of an awareness of the concept of the synodic cycle, but only as an implicit structural feature, because it is nowhere explicitly mentioned and its duration is not quantified by adding up the constitutive intervals of visibility and invisibility.

Tab. 2: Selected Venus data from *Enūma Anu Enlil* Tablet 63 separated by multiples of 8 years.

	cycle 1	cycle 2	cycle 6
evening last	Year 1 Month XI Day 15	Year 3 Month VI Day 23	Year 9 Month III (error for XII) Day 11
morning first	Year 1 Month XI Day 18	Year 3 Month VII Day 13	Year 9 Month XII Day 15
morning last	Year 2 Month VIII Day 11	Year 4 Month IV! Day 2	Year 10 Month VIII Day 10
evening first	Year 2 Month X Day 19	Year 4 Month VI Day 3	Year 10 Month X Day 16

Enūma Anu Enlil Tablet 63 continues with a second sequence comprising twelve omens about Venus phenomena (omens 22–33), which reveals another aspect of the conceptualization of the Venus cycle. The omens in the second sequence employ a similar formulation as those in the first sequence, but the dates are entirely schematic.[7] Each omen covers a portion of a synodic cycle starting from the first appearance in the east or the west, each time in a different month of the schematic year. The following omens for Months I and II are exemplary for the others:

> In Month I Day 2 Venus appears in the east: (…). Until Day 6 of Month IX it stands in the east, Day 7 of Month IX it disappears, 3 months it remains (invisible) in the sky, Day 8 of Month XII Venus rises in the west: (…)
> In Month II Day 3 Venus appears in the west: (…). Until Day 7 of Month X it stands in the west, Day 7 of Month X it disappears, 7 days it remains (invisible) in the sky, Day 15 of Month X Venus rises in the east: (…).

---

6 The correct date Month XI Day 10 for evening last is written in a separate omen. Some deviations may result from scribal errors. Deviations of about one whole month can be ascribed to the irregularities of intercalation, which requires the occasional insertion of a thirteenth month in some years.
7 Hunger and Pingree 1999, 32–39.

The underlying rule is that Venus is visible in the east for 8 months 5 days, invisible for 3 months, visible in the west for 8 months 5 days, invisible for 7 days, then reappears in the east. If we add up the intervals of visibility and invisibility this yields 19 months 17 days for the duration of the entire synodic cycle. This is reasonably close to the actual mean duration,[8] which suggests that the value was derived from empirical reports by averaging in some suitable manner. However, in reality the synodic cycles vary irregularly about a mean value. Another difference with the first sequence is that the omens of the second sequence do not correspond to an astronomically possible sequence of events. They are based on a single rule for the division of the synodic cycle, which is exemplified in twelve analogously constructed statements, one for every month of the schematic year.

A few remarks about the date of *Enūma Anu Enlil* Tablet 63, also known as the *Venus tablet of Ammiṣaduqa*, are necessary. All of the extant manuscripts date after ca. 720 BCE and most scholars assume a similar date of composition as the rest of the series, say 1100–750 BCE. However, some scholars have argued that it preserves data from the Old Babylonian period (ca. 1900–1650 BCE), because the tablet mentions a year formula from the reign of this Old Babylonian king (ca. 1650 BCE).[9] If correct then knowledge of the Venus cycle existed some 800 years earlier than what is suggested by *Mul.Apin*. By implication, the underlying conceptualization of cyclicity would be equally old. However, a date of composition in the first millennium BCE is more plausible. The Venus data may still pertain to the reign of Ammiṣaduqa, in the sense that later scholars reconstructed them by projecting contemporary data into the remote past, a practice that is securely attested on several other tablets from the first millennium BCE (see below).

The intervals of invisibility and visibility of Mercury and Saturn mentioned in *Mul.Apin* are duplicated in AO 6450, a much later tablet from Seleucid Uruk (ca. 200 BCE) inscribed with a commented version of *Enūma Anu Enlil* Tablet 56, which contains planetary omens.[10] The intervals are mentioned in two com-

---

[8] Depending on whether one month is reckoned as 30 days or 29.56 days, 19 months 17 days amounts to 587 days or 578 days, respectively, while the correct mean value is 584 days (Brown 2000, 249–250).

[9] There are numerous studies in which the data on the tablet are used for deriving an absolute chronology of the Old Babylonian period, based on the assumption that the phenomena were observed during the reign of Ammiṣaduqa (e.g. Mebert 2010). However, the Old Babylonian origin of the data is contested (Hunger and Pingree 1999, 37).

[10] For an edition of AO 6450 see Largement 1957. For other manuscripts of *Enūma Anu Enlil* Tablet 56 see Fincke 2015.

mentary sections on the reverse of the tablet. The section regarding Saturn is as follows:[11]

> Saturn, also (called) the Scales, star of the sun, becomes visible in the east, stands in the sky for one year, and disappears in the west. (...) It disappears in the west, remains (invisible) in the sky for 20 days, and rises, becoming visible in the east in the path of the sun.

A comparison with the corresponding statements about Saturn in *Mul.Apin* quoted earlier reveals that the author merged them in chronological order, resulting in a complete description of the synodic cycle from one to the next instance of the first appearance in the east. In between the two parts there is a brief statement which is not translated here, but rendered as (...). It is unclear whether these commentarial additions are unique to AO 6450, or they are also present in earlier manuscripts of *Enūma Anu Enlil* Tablet 56. It seems rather plausible that they were added to *Enūma Anu Enlil* Tablet 56 after ca. 600 BCE, when Babylonian scholars had developed a robust concept of the synodic cycle, which will be described subsequently.

Mul.Apin, *Enūma Anu Enlil* Tablet 63, and the commentary on Tablet 56 contain statements about the invisibility and the visibility of planets and schematic values for the intervals between these phenomena. But the concept of synodic cycle is absent from *Mul.Apin* and only hinted at in *Enūma Anu Enlil* Tablets 56 and 63.[12] The available evidence suggests that by 750 BCE scholars had not yet developed the synodic cycle as a distinct concept and quantified it so that it could be exploited for predictive purposes.[13] Cyclicity was not yet conceived of and quantified in terms of synodic cycles and period relations, but rather represented in lists of the constitutive intervals of visibility and invisibility, as well as lists of dates of successive synodic phenomena that are long enough to illustrate approximate cyclicity through calendar dates that almost repeat. But the underlying rules and cycle durations are not made explicit and must therefore be reconstructed from the lists of intervals.

---

[11] Translation adapted from Largement 1957, 252, lines 96–98. See also Hunger and Steele 2019, 207.
[12] Swerdlow 1998, 26.
[13] Brown 2000, 118.

4 Cyclicity in Babylonian astronomical diaries and related texts (ca. 750 BCE – 75 CE)

After 750 BCE, the astral sciences reached previously unknown levels of sophistication in Babylonia. The developments concerned the scope and the depth of the empirical knowledge of celestial phenomena, the level of theoretical understanding of the underlying regularities, and the methods for predicting them. The two most important bodies of evidence for these developments are the astronomical diaries and related texts (ca. 750 BCE – 75 CE) and the corpus of mathematical astronomy (ca. 400–50 BCE). In each of these corpora we can identify a distinctly new understanding and conceptualization of cyclicity and a new methodology for predicting lunar and planetary phenomena. Moreover, the methods that were developed for predicting astronomical phenomena were also applied to other phenomena. In this manner concepts of cyclicity and predictability were transferred from astral science to other realms of knowledge. The latter developments can be traced through Late Babylonian astrological texts.

4.1 Astronomical diaries, Goal Year methods, and the predictive turn

Most of the extant astronomical diaries and related texts originate from Babylon, where they were produced between the seventh century BCE and the first century CE, apparently without significant interruptions, by astronomers connected to Esagila, the temple of Marduk/Bel. The activities of these scholars are without parallel in the ancient world in terms of their longevity, scope, and complexity. With the onset of the astronomical diaries and related texts, Babylon became the main center of Mesopotamian astral science, a role that it would continue to play until the end of cuneiform.

From very early on, cyclicity was a central concept in the methods of these scholars. Before discussing how they investigated, conceptualized and used astronomical cycles, some further background information must be provided about the astronomical diaries and related texts. They can be divided into several distinct subgenres, each of which contains a particular selection of empirical and/or predicted data. The most common subgenre is half-yearly diaries, which contain reports for half a calendar year of six or seven months arranged in monthly sections.¹ In ordinary years of twelve months, each half-yearly diary covers six months, but in intercalary years, the diary for the second half of the year covers seven months. The Babylonian designation of these texts, *naṣāru ša ginê*, translates as "regular watch". Each half-yearly diary contained a label "regular watch for month MN1 until MN2 of year Y, NN was king", which was usually written on the edge, thus allowing easy retrieval of the tablet from a library shelf. Half-yearly diaries are attested from 561 BCE until 60 BCE, with relatively little change in their structure and content. The following types of phenomena are routinely reported in these texts: astronomical phenomena, weather phenomena, market rates of agricultural commodities, the level of the river Euphrates, local events, and military and political events affecting Babylon. The astronomical phenomena occupy most of the text of each monthly section. They can be divided into six groups:

(1) Normal-Star passages. The scholars reported the dates when the moon and the planets pass by the so-called Normal Stars, a group of about 28 reference stars that straddle the zodiac.² The Babylonian name for these stars, "counting stars", points to their use in measuring and quantifying distances between the moon and the planets from these stars. Usually, the date of passage is reported together with two perpendicular distances expressed in cubits and fingers, Babylonian units of celestial distance, where 1 cubit = 24 fingers ≈ 2.3 modern degrees of arc. One value pertains to the distance "in front of" or "behind" the star, the other value to the distance "above" or "below" the star. Through a statistical analysis of these distances it has been established that the former direction is roughly parallel to the ecliptic and the latter one perpendicular to it, and that "in front of" and "behind" are defined in relation to the daily rising from east to west, i.e. "in front of" means to the west of, and "behind" means to the east of.³ For the moon, which completes one full revolution through the zodiac in about 27 days, Normal Star passages are reported almost daily, for the much more slowly moving planets more rarely, depending on the speed of the planet.

(2) Lunar Six intervals. This modern term designates a set of six time intervals between sunset or sunrise and moonset or moonrise. They were measured and reported on specific days near the beginning, the middle, and the end of each month. The values of these intervals are expressed in the unit UŠ

---

1 For editions of the astronomical diaries and related texts see Sachs and Hunger 1988; Sachs and Hunger 1989; Sachs and Hunger 1996; Hunger 2001; Hunger 2006; Hunger 2014; Hunger 2022. For a recent study of these texts see Haubold, Steele, and Stevens 2019.
2 Jones 2004.
3 Graßhoff 1999; Jones 2004.

(sometimes translated as "time degree"), where 360 UŠ correspond to one day, so that 1 UŠ corresponds to 4 modern minutes. It is not clear how the Lunar Six intervals were measured—perhaps with a water clock. Moreover, a fully satisfying and comprehensive explanation as to why they were routinely reported in the astronomical diaries remains to be found. For the present purpose it suffices to mention one of these intervals, NA_1, for which a plausible explanation can be given. The interval NA_1 is the time between sunset and moonset on the day when the lunar crescent can be seen for the first time, which happens at most a few days after New Moon, i.e. the conjunction of the sun and the moon. This event, the appearance of the new crescent after sunset, marked the beginning of Day 1 of the new month in the Babylonian calendar. After centuries of experience with observing the first crescent, Mesopotamian scholars knew that it can be observed either at the end of Day 29 or Day 30 according to a seemingly irregular pattern. However, the Babylonian scholars found out that visibility of the first crescent is guaranteed if NA_1 exceeds a certain threshold value of typically 10 UŠ or 40 minutes. If NA_1 is larger than this value then the first crescent is bright enough to be visible. By implication the first crescent event is predictable, i.e. whether it will happen on Day 29 or 30, once the value of NA_1 is predictable, which is what the Babylonian astronomers had achieved by about 600 BCE using a cycle-based method (see below).

(3) Synodic phenomena of the planets. As mentioned earlier, they correspond to conspicuous events in the apparent motion of the planets and had been previously identified and observed by Mesopotamian practitioners of celestial divination in earlier centuries. The synodic phenomena form a periodically repeating cycle, which is distinct for Mercury and Venus on the one hand and Mars, Jupiter, and Saturn on the other hand. For the latter three planets, the synodic cycle consists of the first appearance, the first station, the acronychal rising, the second station, and the last appearance, after which the cycle repeats itself. At the first appearance, the planet becomes visible again after a period of invisibility. From then on until the first station the planet moves in the normal, eastward direction along the zodiac. Between the first station and the second station the planet moves in the retrograde, westward direction. Roughly halfway between the stations the planet is in opposition to the sun. That phenomenon is not directly observable, but at most a few days before the opposition the Babylonian scholars observed the planet's acronychal rising, which is the last visible rising in the east after sunset. After the last appearance, the planet is invisible due its apparent proximity to the sun. In the case of Mercury and Venus four synodic phenomena were regularly reported, namely first and last appearances in the west (i.e. in the evening) and the

same in the east (in the morning). These planets also experience stations, but they were only rarely reported. The reported data include the date of the phenomenon and the position of the planet in relation to a Normal Star, or, after about 400 BCE, the zodiacal sign.
(4) After about 400 BCE, each monthly section includes a list of the planets and the zodiacal signs in which they were located in that month. If a planet moved into another sign in the course of the month, then the date of the sign entry is also reported.
(5) Annual phenomena. As opposed to planetary phenomena, which can happen at any date, solar or stellar phenomena occur once per year near fixed dates in the Babylonian calendar. This is true for solstices, equinoxes, and heliacal risings and settings of stars. Each of these events occurs within a certain narrow range of Babylonian calendar dates, depending on the phenomenon. They do not repeat on exactly the same calendar dates in successive years because of the luni-solar nature of the Babylonian calendar.
(6) Lunar and solar eclipses. Eclipse reports are routinely included in the diaries, but they also exist as a distinct genre within the textual family of astronomical diaries and related texts. They include a fixed set of items such as the date, the time of the beginning and the end of the eclipse, the direction of motion of the shadow across the lunar or solar disk, the magnitude and the duration of the eclipse, and accompanying circumstances, such as wind directions, and the visibility of planets during the eclipse.

In addition to the six main groups, more ephemeral astronomical phenomena such as comets and meteors were also occasionally reported. In comparison with the celestial omen tradition, e. g. the series *Enūma Anu Enlil* and *Mul.Apin*, the formulation, the vocabulary, and the content of the astronomical diaries and related text are significantly different. Particularly striking is the consistent use of an extremely terse style of reporting which is devoid of metaphors, ambiguous expressions, and divinatory interpretation. The content is strictly confined to reports of empirical data. However, the selection of the data provides clues about the motivation for their inclusion. For instance, the Lunar Six interval NA_1 points to calendrical applications, while lunar and solar eclipses and synodic phenomena point to astrological applications.

A striking aspect of the reported celestial phenomena is that most of them were predictable by about 600 BCE, when the content and the structure of the half-yearly diaries had stabilized. The predictable phenomena include the mentioned planetary phenomena (Normal Star passages; synodic phenomena), annual phenomena of the sun and the stars, Lunar Six intervals, lunar eclipses, and, after about 500 BCE, also solar eclipses. Apart from explicit evidence in the form of texts and tables with predictions for concrete future years, the existence of predictive methods for these astronomical phenomena is revealed by predictions embedded within the astronomical diaries themselves. These predictions were inserted as replacements for reports of phenomena that were not observed for a variety of reasons. For instance, adverse weather conditions such as clouds or rain could prevent the observation of astronomical phenomena near the horizon. It also happened that no preliminary reports were available for certain dates, perhaps because the astronomer charged with carrying out the watch was unable to do so, or his report was lost. In such cases missing data was replaced by predictions. We know this, because they were explicitly marked with the gloss "not watched for" (NU PAP). Embedded predictions are already attested in the early half-yearly diaries and related reports, such as compilations of Lunar Six data, from ca. 600 BCE onward. In diaries and related texts from earlier years, phenomena are simply omitted or left blank if weather conditions prevented their observation.

Normal Star passages of the moon constitute the only group of astronomical phenomena that were routinely and frequently reported in the astronomical diaries even though they were not predictable within the predictive framework connected to the astronomical diaries and related texts, which is based on Goal Year methods (see below). In the case of adverse weather conditions, reports of the moon's Normal Star passages were not replaced by predictions. After ca. 400 BCE Babylonian astronomers developed zodiac-based mathematical methods for computing the moon's motion, but they were not used for substituting any missing Normal Star passages of the moon in the astronomical diaries. For some other celestial phenomena, such as comets and meteors, the Babylonian scholars did formulate predictive rules (see below), but there is no evidence for concrete predictions made with these rules.

How were the predictions obtained? Those embedded in the astronomical diaries do not readily reveal the underlying method of prediction. But Goal Year texts, Almanacs, and Normal-Star Almanacs, predictive texts closely related to the astronomical diaries, have enabled a virtually complete reconstruction of the underlying method, which is known by the modern term Goal Year method. The underlying principle can be summarized as follows: after a certain period expressed in years, which varies from planet to planet, the phenomena of the planet repeat near the same Babylonian calendar date and near the same Normal Star.[4] In other words, Goal Year periods achieve a close repetition in both the temporal domain and the spatial domain. As we shall see, the underlying concept of cyclic-

---

4 See also Steele 2011a.

ity is a composite one. The most commonly used Goal Year periods are listed in Table 3.

Tab. 3: Commonly used Babylonian Goal Year periods for predicting lunar and planetary phenomena expressed in years, months, synodic cycles, and modern orbital periods.

planet	Goal Year period [years]	synodic months	synodic cycles	orbital periods	predicted phenomena
Moon	18	223	223	241	synodic phenomena, eclipses
Jupiter	71	878	65	6	synodic phenomena
	83	1027	76	7	Normal Star passages
Venus	8	99	5	13	synodic phenomena, Normal Star passages
Mercury	46	567	145	191	synodic phenomena, Normal Star passages
Saturn	59	730	57	2	synodic phenomena, Normal Star passages
Mars	47	581	22	25	Normal Star passages
	79	977	37	42	synodic phenomena

In order to achieve a close return to the same calendar date, the Goal Year periods must correspond to nearly integer numbers of years (Table 3). These numbers of years are frequently mentioned in Babylonian texts. However, a close inspection of the manner in which Goal Year periods are used reveals that the whole numbers of years are actually shorthand for periods reckoned and conceived of in terms of synodic months, with small corrections on top of that expressed in days. For instance, the 8-year period for Venus was actually conceived of as 99 months plus a correction of, at most, a few days. This leads to a minor complication connected to the Babylonian calendar, because 99 months do not always correspond to 8 calendar years due to the variable number of intercalary months that fall within this period. As a consequence, 99 months separate two identical calendar months 8 years apart or two shifted months 8 years apart.

The relation between Goal Year periods and synodic periods can be explained as follows. The synodic phenomena of the planets are first and last appearances and stations, those of the moon are conjunctions and oppositions. Synodic phenomena correspond to specific spatial configurations of the planet or the moon in relation to the sun. The planet or the moon is in conjunction or opposition with, or ahead of or behind the sun by a certain typical angular distance, depending on the synodic phenomenon. The synodic cycle refers to the motion of the planet or the moon from one to the next instance of the same synodic phenomenon, e.g. from first appearance to first appearance. After one synodic cycle the configuration repeats itself, but shifted along the ecliptic at a different celestial position. The distance by which the planet or the moon is shifted along the ecliptic during one synodic cycle is referred to as the synodic arc in modern scholarship. The synodic cycle therefore entails a repetition, but due to the shift it does not in general amount to a suitable period for predicting synodic phenomena. In addition to the fact that the synodic arc does not in general correspond to a whole number of revolutions around the zodiac, there are two other reasons for this. Secondly, the synodic cycle does not produce a close return to the same calendar date for any planet. This is apparent from the fact that they correspond to fractional numbers of years (Table 3). For instance, the synodic cycle of Venus lasts about 1.6 years. Thirdly, individual instances of the synodic cycle for a given planet are of variable duration and the associated synodic arc also varies. For instance, the synodic cycle of Venus has a mean duration of 584 days, during which it covers a mean distance of 575° along the ecliptic. For individual cycles the duration and synodic arc vary around their mean values, an empirical fact also evident in *Enūma Anu Enlil* Tablet 64 (see above). This variability is mainly connected to the planet's location in the zodiac.

The Babylonian scholars in effect solved all three problems simultaneously by constructing Goal Year periods from suitably chosen whole numbers of synodic cycles, such that after one Goal Year period the synodic phenomena repeat near the same Babylonian calendar date and celestial position. In the case of Venus, the Goal Year period of choice contains five synodic cycles, which correspond to about 8 years or 99 months. It is important to note that the three mentioned problems are connected for synodic phenomena. In other words, by adopting a Goal Year period that achieves a repetition of the synodic phenomena near the same calendar dates, the other two problems are also solved, a fact that was understood by the Babylonian scholars. The reason for the interdependence is that, as mentioned, synodic phenomena correspond to specific relative spatial configurations of the planet and the sun, so that the planet or the moon is aligned with, ahead of, or behind the sun by a certain angular distance depending on the synodic phenomenon. After one synodic cycle the configuration repeats itself at a different celestial position with respect to the stars. By repeating the synodic cycle as many times as necessary for achieving a close return to the same calendar date, e.g. five times for Venus corresponding to eight years, the sun completes as many full revolutions around the zodiac as the number of years. It follows that the sun returns to the same celestial position in the absolute sense and, because the relative configuration of sun and planet is the same, the planet also returns to the same celestial position with respect to the stars.

4.1 Astronomical diaries, Goal Year methods, and the predictive turn — 21

In the case of Normal Star passages, the Goal Year period produces a close return of the planet to the same Normal Star near the same Babylonian calendar date. For most planets the Goal Year periods for predicting synodic phenomena were also used for predicting Normal Star passages. This is not surprising, because the planet returns to the same spatial configuration with regard to the fixed stars after one such period, as argued above, so that the Normal Star passages of the planet will also repeat at about the same dates in the Babylonian calendar. For some planets (Jupiter, Mars) distinct Goal Year periods were adopted for the prediction of Normal Star passages. It can be shown that these periods are indeed slightly more accurate for Normal Star passages in the sense that the associated corrections expressed in days, which must be added to the number of months, are smaller than the corrections that would be applied if the Goal Year periods for synodic phenomena would be used. Conversely the latter Goal Year periods are more accurate for synodic phenomena.

The reader may wonder what is the relation between Babylonian Goal Year periods and modern orbital periods, which denote the time that it takes for the planet to carry out a full revolution around the sun with respect to the fixed stars. In the case of Venus, the Goal Year period of 8 years corresponds to 13 orbital periods. Analogous relations exist between Goal Year period and the orbital period for the other planets (Table 3). However, it would be anachronistic to explain the suitability of any Goal Year period by pointing out that it contains a whole number of orbital periods, because the Babylonian scholars did not use the heliocentric framework and they did not know the concept of orbital period, nor did they measure these periods.

It is evident that the Goal Year periods were conceived by scholars who had access to a large body of empirical knowledge of planetary and lunar phenomena. The periods must be viewed as the outcome of some iterative process in which the scholars explored reports of synodic phenomena and Normal Star passages similar to the astronomical diaries and related texts, formulated hypothetical period-based predictive rules, and testing them against the reported data. It is in fact relatively straightforward to recognize in such reports that the Normal Star passages of Venus repeat after five cycles corresponding to 8 years or 99 months. Indeed, certain Babylonian tablets with observational reports for single planets excerpted from diaries are arranged in a tabular layout, probably in order to facilitate the investigation of data separated by Goal Year periods. For example, *ADRT* 5 56 (Hunger 2001) contains Venus data for an interval of 64 years from Artaxerxes I Year 1 through Artaxerxes II Year 4 (464–401 BCE). The table consists of eight columns, each of which contains data for 8 years divided over as many cells separated by rulings. The cells are horizontally aligned, which allows the reader to examine deviations from exact repetition between adjacent cells separated by 8 years. Such tables might well be the source of the corrections expressed in days that were applied to the Goal Year periods reckoned in months.

obverse

Art I 1	9	17	25	33	41	8	16
2	10	18	26	34	Dar II 1	9	17
3	11	19	27	35	2	10	18
4	12	20	28	36	3	11	19

reverse

5	13	21	29	37	4	12	Art II 1
6	14	22	30	38	5	13	2
7	15	23	31	39	6	14	3
8	16	24	32	40	7	15	4

Fig. 1: Tabular layout of the Babylonian tablet *ADRT* 5 56 with reports of synodic phenomena and Normal Star passages of Venus for Artaxerxes I Year 1 through Artaxerxes II Year 4. Source: M. Ossendrijver.

This can be illustrated with reports of the last appearance of Venus contained in the second row on the obverse:

> (Year 2, Month XII$_2$), the 1st, last appearance in the west in Aries.
> (Year 10, Month XII), the 27th, last appearance in the west in Pisces.
> (Year 18, Month XII), the 21st, last appearance in the west in the end of Pisces.
> (Year 26, Month XII), the 18th, last appearance in the west in Pisces.
> (Year 34, Month XII), around the 13th, last appearance in the west in Pisces.

As can be seen, the phenomenon repeats near the same calendar date and celestial position, but the dates recede by several days from one to the next instance separated by eight years or five synodic cycles. Tables like the one shown in Fig. 1 could have been used for determining corrections expressed in days that had to be applied to the dates in the context of the Goal Year method. The same phenomenon can also be observed with the Normal Star passages, for instance the following two from the fourth row on the obverse:

> (Year 4, Month IV), the 26th, it (Venus) was balanced 2/3 cubit above the Bright Star of the Furrow
> (Year 12, Month IV), the 24th, it was 1/2 cubit [above the Bright Star] of the Furrow.

The Bright Star of the Furrow is a Normal Star identified with α Virginis, also known as Spica. Like its synodic phenomena, the passages of Venus by this star repeat near the same date after 8 years reckoned in months.

4.2 Goal Year methods and their conceptualization in procedure texts

Having discussed some basic properties of Goal Year periods, the investigation continues with an exploration of several procedure texts for predicting planetary phenomena using Goal Year periods. They are preserved on Late Babylonian tablets from Babylon and Uruk, the main centers of Babylonian astral science in the Late Babylonian period. The tablets most likely originate from temple libraries and/or private libraries of priestly scholars who were active in the astral sciences. A few general remarks about procedure texts as a genre of Mesopotamian scholarly texts are necessary in order to contextualize the Goal Year procedures and other Late Babylonian procedure texts that operate with conceptions of cyclicity. The Mesopotamian genre of procedure texts can be traced back to the early second millennium BCE. In the first millennium BCE such texts are attested in many different realms of scholarship and daily life, including the astral sciences, mathematics, healing practices, rituals, and the cult. In the astral sciences, procedure texts became especially important in the second half of the first millennium BCE, when scholars developed increasingly complex computational methods for predicting celestial phenomena. Procedure texts are usually compendia with multiple instructions formulated in the second person for carrying out certain operations. Usually no justifications or explanations of the instructions are included. Moreover, it is not always clear how and when a procedure was meant to be executed or, in the case of compendia with alternative procedures, how to choose between them. This suggests that the use of procedure texts was accompanied by oral instructions from master to pupil.

With that in mind it is instructive to explore several Goal Year procedures and investigate how Goal Year periods, and cyclicity in general, are conceptualized in these texts. The following two passages from compendia with Goal Year procedures are concerned with the synodic phenomena of Venus. They are taken from BM 34560 and BM 45728, Late Babylonian tablets from Babylon (ca. 500–100 BCE) kept in the British Museum:[5]

> The setting and appearance of Venus: in 8 years you subtract 4 days.
> [The appearances] of Venus: 8 years you turn back behind you, you diminish [your year] by 4 days, it appears.

In the first passage, "setting" and "appearance" are abbreviated terms for the planet's last appearance in the morning or evening and the first appearance in the morning or evening, respectively. In the second passage only "appearances" are mentioned. However, tablets with concrete predictions (Goal Year texts, Almanacs) reveal that for a given planet the same rule was applied to all synodic phenomena. It follows that "setting and appearance" and "appearances" can represent, *pars pro toto*, any synodic phenomenon. Both procedures express the same Goal Year rule for Venus phenomena, albeit in slightly different ways. An interesting aspect of the second passage is the instruction to turn back 8 years, which refers to the act of retrieving reports of phenomena ("appearances") preceding the Goal Year by the Goal Year period (8 years) from existing records, i. e. astronomical diaries and related texts, and applying a correction expressed in days to the dates thus obtained (in this case -4 days). A comparison with the Venus records in *ADRT* 5 56 quoted above reveals that this correction is roughly in agreement with empirical facts. It is important to note that the correction is conceived of and applied in relation to a Goal Year period defined as a whole number of months (99) and not as a whole number of years (8). In that sense the formulation adopted by the Babylonian scholars combines convenience of expression with astronomical accuracy.

The following Late Babylonian procedure text VAT 17343, which was excavated in Babylon, preserves fragments of Goal Year rules for predicting the synodic phenomena of the planets:[6]

---

5 First passage: BM 34560 obv. 8; for a copy of this tablet see *LBAT* 1515; no edition has been published. Second passage: BM 45728 obv. 5–6 (Britton 2002, 59–61).
6 VAT 17343 (unpublished), excavated by R. Koldewey in archive N19, kept in the Vorderasiatisches Museum (Berlin). This tablet will be published in collaboration with Prof. Kristin Kleber and the project "GoviB – Governance in Babylon: Negotiating the Rule of Three Empires" (ERC Consolidator Grant No. 10100619).

4.2 Goal Year methods and their conceptualization in procedure texts — 25

> [… Jupiter …] 71 years: day (corresponds) to day.
> [… Venus …] 8 years: you subtract 4 days.
> [… Mercury …] 46 years: day (corresponds) to day.
> [… Saturn …] 59 years: you subtract 5 days.
> [… Mars …] 79 years: day (corresponds) to day.

They can be identified with the Goal Year periods for synodic phenomena from Table 3. The planets are listed in the Babylonian astrological order from Jupiter, the most benefic planet, to Mars, the most malefic planet. The rule for Venus coincides with those mentioned on BM 34560 and BM 45728 (see above). The prediction of Normal Star ("counting star") passages with Goal Year periods is also covered by Late Babylonian procedure texts. One example is the compendium BM 41004, which includes the following rules:[7]

> The passings of Venus with the "counting stars": in 12 years 4 days are lacking to your year. Alternatively in 16 years 2 days are lacking to your year (…)
> In 8 years the position of Venus recedes by 4 degrees. (…)
>
> The passings of Mars with the "counting stars": in 32 years 4 days are lacking to your year. Alternatively: in 47 years 4 days are lacking to your year. (…)
>
> The passings of Saturn with the "counting stars": in 59 years 6 days are lacking to your year. (…)
>
> The passings of Mercury with the "counting stars": in 13 years 3 days are lacking to your year.
> In 46 years 1 day is lacking to your year (…).
> In 2,6 (= 126) years day (corresponds) to day, it appears.

These procedures reveal several additional features of the Goal Year method and its conceptualization. The expression "your year", which also occurred in the passage from BM 45728 quoted above, is a characteristic element of Goal Year procedures. It is not found in earlier Mesopotamian instructional texts, neither in the astral sciences, nor in other realms of knowledge. "Your year" refers to the Goal Year, say Y, for which the user intends to make a prediction. It constitutes the starting point from which the user turns back by the Goal Year period, say P years (in actual practice a fixed number of months). The turning back from year Y by P years refers to the act of consulting existing astronomical diaries for year Y-P and retrieving the relevant quotations about the planet and the phenomenon under consideration. This act constitutes the beginning of a transformation from reports of synodic phenomena and Normal Star passages contained in

---

[7] BM 41004 rev. 5–6, 8, 10–11, 13, 16–18. For an edition see Brack-Bernsen and Hunger 2005–06.

astronomical diaries for year Y-P into predictions for year Y. As indicated by the procedure texts, this transformation may involve adding or subtracting a certain number of days to the date retrieved from the diary.

BM 41004 is one of several procedure texts that list additional Goal Year periods beyond the standard ones from Table 3. The alternative periods for the same planet can be shorter or longer than the standard one. It is revealing that they are listed on tablets, even though the predictive texts (Goal Year texts; Almanacs) suggest that only one of them was actually used. It seems plausible that the scholars had compared different rules for each planet and selected one of them based on pragmatic considerations of accuracy, the size of the correction to the dates, i.e. the smaller the better, and practicality, e.g. periods shorter than about 100 years are preferred. This is consistent with the suggestion made above that the Goal Year rules were constructed in some iterative process involving the analysis of records such as *ADRT* 5 56. However, the alternative rules were not discarded. One possible reason for this that they could be used if an astronomical diary needed for making predictions with the standard rule, i.e. the diary for year Y-P, was lacking for some reason. In that case the alternative rule would allow the user to make the predictions by consulting reports from an astronomical diary for a different year. In the case of Venus, the 16-year period would enable the use of data from year Y-16 instead of Y-8. It is interesting to note that the alternative periods are usually not simple multiples of another period for the same planet. Secondly, they are often listed systematically in order of increasing length, such that the longest one produces an exact return to the same date ("day corresponds to day"), while the shorter periods require corrections to the date. It follows that the scholars had developed a sophisticated understanding of the concept of cyclicity which allowed for the cyclical behavior of one and the same phenomenon to be described and predicted with different, alternative and non-equivalent period-based models, each featuring a different period and a different correction expressed in days.

Until now the present discussion of the Goal Year methods has focused on the planets, but such methods were also developed for lunar phenomena, in particular eclipses and Lunar Six intervals. In both cases the scholars used a Goal Year period of 223 months, known in modern scholarship as the saros cycle. Disregarding occasional shifts of one month caused by the vagaries of intercalation, this cycle corresponds to 18 years, which is how the Babylonian scholars labeled it. Eclipses were predicted by essentially the same method as planetary phenomena, that is, eclipses reported in the year preceding the Goal Year by 18 years (223 months) were projected into the Goal Year and a certain constant correction was applied. In this case the correction affects the time of the eclipse, which is shifted by 1/3 of a day between eclipses separated by 223 months, roughly in agreement with empirical facts. But the Goal Year methods for Lunar Six intervals are more complex than those for planetary phenomena and eclipses. An almost complete reconstruction of these methods was achieved in the 1990s by Lis Brack-Bernsen.[8] Analogously to planetary phenomena and lunar eclipses, the prediction of a Lunar Six interval starts with copying the value of that quantity for the month preceding the goal month by 223 months. A novelty concerns the corrections which are applied, because they are not constant but variable, being computed from the sum of two other Lunar Six intervals for the month preceding the goal month by 229 months. As shown by Brack-Bernsen, these intricate and non-obvious Goal Year algorithms for the Lunar Six intervals are essentially correct by modern standards. This implies that the Babylonian scholars derived them in some iterative process by analyzing records of measured Lunar Six intervals, identifying patterns in these records, formulating hypothetical predictive rules, testing these rules, and correcting them if necessary. The available Babylonian sources mainly inform us about the endpoint of this process. But it seems plausible that conveniently formatted tables of Lunar Six data similar to the Jupiter table in Fig. 1 were used for this.

4.3 Reflections on the use of cyclicity in the astronomical diaries and related texts

The Goal Year methods also provide a partial answer to the question of why Babylonian scholars reported mainly predictable astronomical phenomena in the astronomical diaries, and why they continued to produce the diaries in an essentially unchanged fashion for many centuries, until the very end of cuneiform culture. It is apparent that an important purpose of the astronomical diaries was to provide the necessary data for generating predictions of the reported phenomena. Since the Goal Year method operates by projecting reported past phenomena into the future by adding the appropriate Goal Year periods, there is a one-to-one correspondence between predictions and past instances of the phenomena reported in the astronomical diaries. In the absence of such reports, the phenomena could not be predicted for future dates with this method. The availability of an uninterrupted sequence of astronomical diaries with full coverage of the astronomical phenomena is a condition for the prediction of these phenomena with the Goal Year method. Therefore, ideally no instance of them was allowed to be missing from the records. This explains why within the diaries themselves reports

---

8 Brack-Bernsen 1997; Brack-Bernsen and Hunger 2002.

of phenomena that could not be observed, usually due to bad weather, were replaced by predictions, accompanied by the gloss "not watched for". These predictions were most likely obtained with the Goal Year method, so that in such cases we can speak of two stages of Goal Year based prediction as being applied in succession.

The fact that reports of phenomena that could not be observed were replaced by predictions indicates that observation and prediction were intertwined activities for the scholars who produced the astronomical diaries. Most of the astronomical phenomena that are reported in the diaries were predictable with Goal Year methods. The relationship between observation and prediction was active in two directions. Not only were Goal Year predictions derived from reported observations, but conversely the observations of lunar and planetary phenomena were guided by Goal Year predictions. The scholars already knew in advance which phenomena were expected on which days, and where they would occur in the sky. This is proven by the existence of tablets with predictions that were derived from astronomical diaries with the help of Goal Year methods, namely Goal Year texts, Almanacs, and Normal Star Almanacs. For reasons that are still unclear it is only in the Seleucid and Parthian periods (after ca. 250 BCE) that all of these genres are attested in Babylon, but it is assumed that the underlying practices were already in place by ca. 600 BCE.[9] The production of the astronomical diaries and related texts and the role of Goal Year based predictions can be visualized as a cyclical process (Fig. 2).

The first genre of predictive texts to be mentioned are Goal Year texts, which are attested from the third century BCE onwards.[10] They contain predictions for the Goal Year in the form of direct quotations of planetary and lunar reports that were copied from half-yearly astronomical diaries. For the moon and each planet data were excerpted from astronomical diaries preceding the Goal Year by the appropriate period from Table 3. For instance, synodic phenomena and Normal Star passages of Venus were copied from diaries for year Y−8, synodic phenomena of Jupiter from diaries for year Y−71, its Normal Star passages from diaries for year Y−83, lunar and solar eclipses from diaries for year Y−18, and Lunar Six data from diaries for years Y−18 and Y−19. However, Goal Year texts represent an intermediate stage in the production of predictions from diary reports. Goal Year texts contain separate sections for each planet and the moon. Within each section the data are arranged chronologically, so that the predictions for a given month have to be collected from multiple sections. Secondly, the Babylonian

---

9 For the historical development of the diaries see Steele 2019.
10 For editions of the Goal Year texts, see Hunger 2006.

4.3 Reflections on the use of cyclicity in the astronomical diaries and related texts

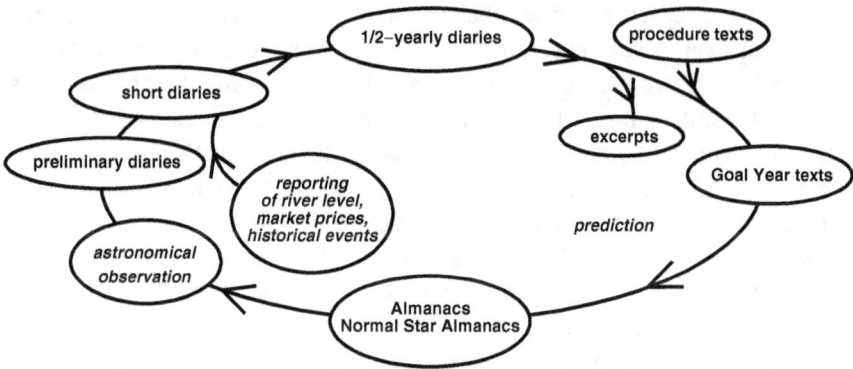

Fig. 2: Production cycle underlying the astronomical diaries and related texts. Source: Ossendrijver 2024.

calendar features ordinary years with twelve months, as well as intercalary years with thirteen months. The number of intercalary years that occur within a given Goal Year interval of P years can vary. It may therefore happen that month M in year Y-P does not correspond to month M, but to month M-1 or M+1 in the Goal Year Y. A mismatch between the months of year Y-P and the months of the Goal Year Y is guaranteed if year Y-P is ordinary while year Y is intercalary, or vice versa. Thirdly, the reports of planetary and lunar phenomena that were copied onto the Goal Year text still include accompanying remarks about weather phenomena, even though they were not considered to be as predictable with the same Goal Year periods as the planetary and lunar phenomena which they accompany.

All three issues were resolved during a next stage of data processing. In this stage two kinds of predictive texts, known in modern scholarship as Almanacs and Normal Star Almanacs, were produced from the Goal Year texts.[11] Like Goal Year texts, they contain predictions for one calendar year. Each Almanac or Normal Star Almanac is produced from data in one Goal Year text, but they are rearranged in strict chronology by the months of the Goal Year. Furthermore, the original months in which the phenomena occurred, as reported in the Goal Year text, are replaced by shifted months in the Goal Year if necessary. Thirdly,

---

11 See Hunger 2014 for editions of the almanacs and Normal Star almanacs. On the relationship between Goal Year texts, Almanacs and Normal Star Almanacs, see Hunger 1999; Hunger and Pingree 1999, 139–182; Gray and Steele 2008; Gray and Steele 2009. The exact procedures by which almanacs and Normal Star almanacs were compiled from Goal Year texts and other sources have yet to be reconstructed.

accompanying reports about weather phenomena were deleted. Fourthly, small corrections expressed in days similar to those prescribed in the procedure texts discussed above, were added to, or subtracted from the dates. Fifthly, the planetary and lunar data are reshuffled and arranged in strict chronology in twelve or thirteen monthly sections. As to the purpose of these predictions, it can be assumed that an important one was to offer guidance to the scholars who carried out the watch and produced the astronomical diaries. As opposed to observing the sky cluelessly and writing reports about whatever phenomena happened to catch their attention, the scholars were thoroughly prepared based on the predictions contained in both types of almanacs.

As mentioned earlier, some celestial phenomena were not predictable with Goal Year methods and are therefore lacking from the Almanacs and Normal Star Almanacs. This concerns the Normal Star passages of the moon, and the appearance of comets. Also, weather phenomena such as rain, clouds, winds, thunder, lightning, and flooding, and terrestrial phenomena such as market rates and historical events, are absent from these predictive texts. Even though they were not considered to be predictable in the same manner as planetary and lunar phenomena, textual evidence to be discussed below proves that Babylonian scholars did develop cycle-based predictive methods for most of these phenomena.

A comparison between the Neo-Assyrian sources and the Late Babylonian sources discussed above reveals significant developments in the knowledge, the understanding, and the conceptualization of astronomical cycles. Compositions such as *Mul.Apin* and *Enūma Anu Enlil* Tablet 56 testify to quantitative knowledge of the constitutive intervals of cyclical planetary motion, but the concept of synodic cycle is absent from these texts, except as an implicit structural element in lists of planetary phenomena. The duration of the synodic cycle is neither conceptualized nor computed from the sum of its constitutive intervals. It is only with the emergence of Goal Year methods in Babylonia (ca. 600 BCE) that planetary cycles are quantified, mentioned explicitly, and incorporated in predictive rules. What can we say about the underlying concept of cyclicity? Goal Year periods are composite cycles in the sense that they contain multiple synodic cycles in order to achieve a close return in the spatial and temporal domains. The Goal Year instructions explicitly link future instances of specific phenomena, such as synodic phenomena and Normal Star passages, to earlier instances of the same phenomena. Their future instances are, in some sense, viewed as repetitions of past instances of the same phenomena. In other words, predictability is conceptualized in terms of periodic repetition. This amounts to a new understanding of both predictability and periodicity. The use of cycles as intervals of repetition is applied very literally in Goal Year texts, which contain reported phenomena copied from diaries but repurposed as predictions.

4.3 Reflections on the use of cyclicity in the astronomical diaries and related texts

These innovations are expressions of the predictive turn in Babylonian astral science. With the introduction of Goal Year methods, prediction became an important goal of astronomical practice. In earlier periods the focus was not on prediction, but on the divinatory interpretation of celestial phenomena as they occurred. As will become apparent in the next section, the state of knowledge, the conceptualization, and the role of planetary cycles underwent further developments in mathematical astronomy (ca. 400–50 BCE). The underlying periods are longer and empirically more accurate, but they are not direct tools of prediction as in the Goal Year method, or even starting points for the predictive algorithms. Instead, the underlying periods are secondary properties of the algorithms.

5 Cyclicity in Babylonian mathematical astronomy (ca. 400–50 BCE)

The introduction of the uniform zodiac in Babylonia near the end of the fifth century BCE led to major developments in the astral sciences with repercussions far beyond Mesopotamia. The uniform zodiac denotes a division of the path of the sun, i.e. the ecliptic, into twelve equal segments of 30 units equivalent to the modern degree of arc. Each segment, i.e. zodiacal sign, was named after a nearby constellation, from the Hired Man (Aries) to the Tails (Pisces). A major development connected with the zodiac is the emergence of mathematical astronomy as a new technique for predicting lunar and planetary phenomena.[1] Babylonian mathematical astronomy is based on much longer and more precise cycles than the Goal Year periods. This involved fundamental changes in the role of cycles for astronomical prediction and in the conceptualization of cyclicity. Cuneiform tablets with mathematical astronomy are attested in Babylon and Uruk between ca. 380 BCE and 50 BCE, a period overlapping with the Achaemenid era (380–331 BCE), the reign of Alexander the Great and his dynasty (330–312 BCE), the Seleucid era (311–146 BCE), and the Parthian era (145–50 BCE). The tablets from Babylon cover this entire period, while the sources from Uruk are fewer and cease near 170 BCE. The scholars who wrote these texts were priests employed by the main temple in either city. Those in Babylon belonged to the same circle of scholars as the authors of the astronomical diaries, which implies that they were familiar with Goal Year methods. The corpus of mathematical astronomy includes procedure texts with rules for making predictions and tablets with concrete predictions for future dates, as they exist for the Goal Year methods.[2] In the case of mathematical astronomy, the products of prediction are computed tables with dates and longitudes of planetary or lunar phenomena and other quantities pertaining to the phenomena.

In mathematical astronomy the uniform zodiac functions as a coordinate frame for expressing and computing positions of the moon, the sun, and the five planets. Celestial positions could henceforth be specified by two complementary coordinates. First, a zodiacal sign and number of degrees within it, secondly, the distance by which the wandering body is above or below the ecliptic. The latter quantity was computed mainly for the moon and was usually ignored for the

---

[1] For a short introduction to Babylonian mathematical astronomy see Ossendrijver 2015.
[2] For and edition and investigation of the procedure texts see Ossendrijver 2012; for the planetary tables see Ossendrijver in press; for the lunar tables see Neugebauer 1955.

planets; it is only for the moon that the computed tables include columns for this quantity. A second novel feature of Babylonian mathematical astronomy is the use of sexagesimal place value notation, not only as a tool for computation, but also for expressing numbers in a written form. In this notation, which has belonged to the computational toolbox of Mesopotamian scribes since about 2100 BCE, numbers are represented as sequences of digits, each having a value between zero and fifty-nine. Every digit is associated with a power of sixty that decreases in the rightward direction. In the Late Babylonian period a special sign was added for indicating vanishing digits (0) within a sexagesimal number. The cuneiform notation for sexagesimal numbers is referred to as floating, because it lacks a sign like our decimal point to mark the beginning of the fractional part of a number. Moreover, vanishing digits at the beginning or the end of a sexagesimal number were not written. The cuneiform notation is therefore ambiguous with regard to the magnitude of numbers and the power of sixty corresponding to each digit can only be inferred from the context. In Babylonian astronomical texts there is nearly always sufficient context to achieve this. In translations, sexagesimal numbers of which the absolute value is known are conventionally rendered by inserting a semicolon (;) between the digit pertaining to 1 and the next digit pertaining to 1/60, and commas between all other digits.

The tables of mathematical astronomy were computed from left to right and from top to bottom like modern spreadsheets. Each column contains a different astronomical quantity, in particular dates and zodiacal positions (longitudes), and their line-by-line differences. The correspondence of the rows depends on the type of table. In synodic tables, which constitute the most common type of table, successive rows pertain to instances of the same synodic phenomenon. That is, the different synodic phenomena of each planet are, in principle, isolated from one another and their dates and zodiacal longitudes are computed independently in separate columns. In addition, the scholars computed tables with daily positions of the planets in between the synodic phenomena. In these so-called daily motion tables successive rows pertain to successive days. Common to both types of tables is that after writing down the initial values in the first row of the table, the rest is filled by updating the columns in the downward direction. Updating refers to the addition or the subtraction of a difference to the value in the preceding row. As opposed to the Goal Year method, where predictions are generated by projecting reported phenomena into the future across Goal Year periods, the methods of mathematical astronomy generate predictions by means of iterative updating. In principle it is possible to generate arbitrarily long sequences of predictions in this manner. The temporal scope of the predictions is therefore much larger than with Goal Year methods. In synodic tables, the central difference quantities used for updating are the synodic arc, which is the longitudinal distance covered by the planet in one synodic cycle, and the synodic time, which is the corresponding time interval. In rough agreement with empirical facts, the Babylonian scholars modeled these differences as periodically varying number sequences, for which they developed several mathematical methods. According to the method known as system B, they are modeled as zigzag sequences, whereby a number goes up and down between two extrema with a constant difference. According to the method known as system A, they are modeled as step functions of longitude, that is, they equal different constant values in different parts of the zodiac. For most planets, several variants of these systems are available.

5.1 Developments in the knowledge and the conceptualization of astronomical cycles

The zodiacal longitudes that are computed with the methods of mathematical astronomy satisfy period relations, such that the planet or the moon returns to exactly the same longitude after a certain number, Π, of synodic cycles. In the course of Π synodic cycles the planet or the moon carries out a certain whole number, Z, of full revolutions around the zodiac, which takes Y years, i.e. revolutions of the sun. Each planetary or lunar algorithm is characterized by a period relation of this kind (Tab. 4).[3] It is important to note that the periods Π, Z, and Y correspond to emic Babylonian concepts, because they are often mentioned in procedure texts. Like the Goal Year periods, the periods in mathematical astronomy contain whole numbers (Π) of synodic cycles. To some extent the development with respect to Goal Year periods is incremental, because the periods are longer and more accurate in relation to the empirical data. But the underlying notion of cyclicity has evolved in more fundamental ways. In order to illustrate the latter changes, it is instructive to consider a simple example. According to system A_0 for the planet Venus, the longitudes of its synodic phenomena are updated with a constant synodic arc of $3,35;30°$ in the sexagesimal place value notation, corresponding to $215.5°$ in the decimal notation. The underlying period relation can

---

[3] The period Z is the number of revolutions produced by Π synodic arcs. The Babylonian term for Z is *palû* (bala), literally "turn" (Ossendrijver 2012, 597), known as the word for "reign" in the *Sumerian King List* and many other texts (see above). The synodic arc is defined as a net longitudinal displacement, i.e. distance traveled along the ecliptic modulo $360°$. Some planets (Venus, Mars) and the moon carry out an additional revolution for each synodic arc, so that the number of revolutions of the planet corresponding to Π synodic arcs is $\Pi+Z$. See also Ossendrijver 2012, 60–61.

5.1 Developments in the knowledge and the conceptualization of astronomical cycles

be expressed as follows: 720 (=Π) synodic cycles correspond to 431 (=Z) revolutions around the zodiac, which take place in 1151 (=Y) years. Compared with the Goal Year period of 8 years, the latter period is much longer, and the same is true for many other planetary periods in mathematical astronomy (Table 4).[4] In particular, 1151 years exceeds the entire timespan of the astronomical diaries, which rules out any possibility of using it as a Goal Year period. Furthermore, this period cannot have been discovered through a comparison of diary reports separated by 1151 years, because there were no such reports. Instead, it was most likely constructed from a shorter period. A plausible scenario becomes evident if we consider five synodic cycles, corresponding to about 8 years, which amount to a longitudinal distance of 5 x 215.5° = 3 x 360° − 2.5°. In other words, five synodic cycles yield a close return to the same longitude, except for a small deviation of -2.5°.[5] In order to obtain 1151 years, it is sufficient to know this deviation, which could be achieved by comparing phenomena 8 years apart only, and compute how many multiples of five cycles it takes for the individual deviations to add up to a full revolution of 360°, namely 360/2.5 = 144. This is sufficient to conclude that an exact return will happen after 8 x 144 − 1 = 1151 years. We can therefore conclude that mathematical astronomy brought a new twist to the conceptualization of cyclicity in comparison with the Goal Year methods. The periods underlying mathematical astronomy achieve an exact return of the planet's synodic phenomena to the same longitude, but they do so as a consequence of the mathematical model for the synodic arc (distanced travelled along the zodiac) and the synodic time (the corresponding time interval), which replace periods as the primary tools of prediction. The exact returns after Π synodic cycles that are produced by the algorithms could in general not be observed, because they occur beyond the timespan of the astronomical diaries. In this manner the concept of cyclicity was extended from Goal Year periods, which connect actual phenomena within the timespan of the astronomical diaries, to much longer, empirically more accurate theoretical periods that were constructed by analyzing deviations from shorter periods.

---

[4] More comprehensive overviews of the period relations used in Babylonian mathematical astronomy can be found in Aaboe 1965 and Neugebauer 1975, 423.
[5] In fact the tablet BM 41004 quoted above includes a statement about the longitudinal deviation of Venus after 8 years, which is said to be -4°.

Tab. 4: Periods of selected algorithms of Babylonian mathematical astronomy (ca. 350–50 BCE).

planet	system	Π [synodic cycles]	Z [revolutions]	Y [years]	predicted phenomena
Moon	A	2783	225	225	synodic phenomena
Jupiter	A, A', B	391	36	427	synodic phenomena
Venus	A_0	720	431	1151	some synodic phenomena
Mercury	A_1	1513	480	480	evening first
	A_1	2673	848	848	morning first
Saturn	A	256	9	265	synodic phenomena
Mars	A, B	133	18	284	some synodic phenomena

6 Planetary conjunctions in Babylonian astral science

Most of the Babylonian periods that have been discussed thus far describe the cyclical behavior of spatial configurations of one planet or the moon in relation to the sun. For instance, the synodic phenomenon of first appearance pertains to the first visible rising of a planet shortly before sunrise, which occurs when it has reached a typical, more or less fixed elongation (longitudinal distance) from the sun. Van der Waerden 1957 introduced the term "solar distance principle" for this property of all synodic phenomena, which is at least approximately satisfied by the Babylonian algorithms. Similarly, the synodic phenomena of the moon, i.e. full moon and new moon, correspond to oppositions and conjunctions of moon and sun, which are well-defined relative configurations of these bodies. The properties of synodic cycles, i.e. their duration and the distances travelled by the planet or the moon and the sun, are consequences of the combined motion of the two bodies, so that the synodic cycle is technically a composite cycle. For the same reason, the 223-month saros cycle, which governs lunar and solar eclipses, is also a composite cycle. But the saros cycle also produces a return of two other periodic components of lunar motion. First, it corresponds to 242 draconitic months, the period in which the moon returns to the same latitude, i.e. distance from the ecliptic. Secondly, it corresponds to 239 so-called anomalistic months, the period in which the moon's varying velocity along the ecliptic returns to the same value.

These considerations raise the question of whether Babylonian scholars also conceived of and quantified periods for the repetition of spatial configurations of two planets, or of one planet and the moon. The answer to this question is of considerable interest, because the Greco-Roman concept of the Great Year is usually defined in terms of the alignment or conjunction of all known planets. Conjunctions between two planets are potential intermediate steps towards the notion of the alignment of all planets. Planetary conjunctions were a major topic of interest for Late Babylonian scholars, primarily in the context of efforts to develop cycle-based methods for predicting non-astronomical phenomena. In addition to the evidence discussed in the present section, planetary conjunctions also feature prominently in new types of procedures for predicting weather phenomena and market rates (Section 7.2) and in cryptographic omens with predictions for king and country (Section 7.6).

6.1 Periods for planetary conjunctions in procedure texts

Quantitative, explicit textual references to periods for planetary conjunctions are very rare in the Babylonian sources. The only known example is BM 76488, a tablet inscribed with a compendium about diverse aspects of astral science.[1] It was probably written near the middle of the first millennium BCE and probably originates from a northern Babylonian city (Sippar, Borsippa, or Babylon). The heavily damaged obverse contains Goal Year procedures for the synodic phenomena of the planets, while the better-preserved reverse contains astrological sections and statements about planetary conjunctions, including detailed knowledge of cycles for planetary conjunctions. It is significant that these astronomical and astrological topics are combined on a single tablet. The sections about conjunctions form two distinct groups. The first group deals with conjunctions from what appears to be an astrological and numerological perspective. It includes the following examples (rev. i 5'–10'):

> Mercury to Saturn sixty years.
> 6 times 10 is 1,(0) (=60).
> 30 times 2 is 1,(0).
>
> Mercury to Mars sixty years.
> 15 times 4 is 1,(0).
> 6 times 10 is 1,(0).

The 60 years assigned to Mercury and Saturn and to Mercury and Mars are not astronomically valid periods for conjunctions between these planets. Furthermore, the multiplications that follow these statements do not correspond to astronomically meaningful relations either. The expressions in the first group must therefore be based on other considerations, presumably of an astrological and/ or a numerological nature. The fact that both periods amount to 1 in floating sexagesimal place value notation points to the latter. However, both periods of 60 years contain valid periods of the involved planets, but in a hidden manner. In the case of Mercury and Saturn 60 can be decomposed as 1 + 59, where 59 years is the standard Goal Year period for Saturn and 1 year is a valid, though unattested Goal Year period for Mercury. In the case of Mercury and Mars 60 can be decomposed as 13 + 47, where 47 years is the standard Goal Year period for Normal Star passages of Mars and 13 years is a valid, but non-standard Goal Year period for Mercury's synodic phenomena. For each conjunction in the first group a decomposition of this kind can be made, which is probably not a coincidence.

---

[1] See Ossendrijver 2017.

However, the Goal Year periods of two different planets do not add up to an astronomically meaningful period for conjunctions between them. If these implicit additions are correctly identified they must express some sort of a hidden connection, perhaps numerological or astrological, between the involved planets.

The tablet continues with a second group of statements in which periods and other primarily numerical data are assigned to pairs of planets in a different manner than in the first group. Much of the latter data defies interpretation and is ignored here, but some of the periods turn out to match astronomically correct Goal Year periods for the repetition of planetary conjunctions near the same calendar date and celestial position, for instance (rev. ii 2', 8', 14', 16'):

Saturn to Jupiter 20 (years): ⌜50?⌝ [days the deficit (?)]
Saturn to Venus 32 (years), 20 days the excess. 59 (years), ⌜6?⌝ days⌝ the deficit (...)
Saturn to Mars 30 (years); 5 (days) the excess (...).
Mercury to Mars 32 (years), 5 (days) the excess (...).

The period of 20 years amounts to a correct mean period for the repetition of conjunctions between Saturn and Jupiter. It is the shortest possible such period, containing one elementary period for conjunctions between these planets.[2] According to modern data it corresponds to 247 synodic months and a subtractive correction of about 41 days, roughly compatible with the 50 days mentioned in the text. Successive conjunctions of Saturn and Jupiter are displaced by about -117°, which results in a close return after three conjunctions or 60 years. The latter period is not attested in Babylonian sources, but it played an important role in the astrology of Māshā'allāh, a Persian Jewish scholar at the Abbasid court in Baghdad (see below). The period of 32 years for conjunctions of Saturn and Venus contains 31 elementary periods for such conjunctions. It does not produce a particularly close return to the same date and celestial position, but neither does any shorter period. Similarly, the period of 30 years assigned to Saturn and Mars contains 15 elementary periods for such conjunctions and is the shortest one that yields a reasonably close return to the same calendar date. Finally, 32 years is a valid period for close returns of conjunctions between Mercury and Mars to the same calendar date, comprising 15 elementary periods for such conjunctions. All of these periods can, in principle, be used for predicting conjunctions by means of the Goal Year method. While this tablet remains, in parts, difficult to interpret, the sections about planetary conjunctions reflect a broader development in Late Babylonian astral science.

---

2 See Ossendrijver 2017.

6.2 Conjunctions in Babylonian astrological historiography

In addition to celestial phenomena (Section 4.1), the astronomical diaries also report local and political events in Babylon in a separate paragraph in each monthly section. The systematic juxtaposition of celestial and historical data indicates that the Babylonian scholars considered them to be connected in some manner.[3] It appears that conjunctions between planets were identified as an important class of phenomena that could signify political developments. This is suggested by Babylonian investigations of conjunctions between planets preserved in planetary excerpts, which are related to the astronomical diaries. The excerpt BM 32209 (*ADRT* 5 58) lists reports of conjunctions of Mars and the moon on the obverse and of conjunctions of Saturn and the moon on the reverse for several years in the 5th and 4th centuries BCE, for example (obv. 5–9):

> Year 2 (of Darius, son of Artaxerxes, son of Xerxes), Month IV, the 23rd, last part of the night, the moon was 2 1/2 cubits below Mars.
> Month V, the 22nd, last part of the night, the moon was 2 cubits below Mars.
> Month VIII , the 19th, last part of the night, the moon was balanced 2 cubits below Mars.
> Month XI, the 12th day, first part of the night, the moon was [....] cubits behind Mars.
> Month XII, the 9th, first part of the night, the moon was 1 cubit in front of Mars.

Since similar reports are contained in half-yearly diaries, there is no doubt that they were the source of such excerpts. The purpose of these excerpts is not entirely clear. It seems possible that they were created in order to investigate conjunctions with the aim of formulating Goal Year type rules for predicting them. But an astrological purpose is also plausible. In particular, the tablet could have been used for interpreting unfavorable events in the past, e.g. political developments affecting Babylonia or private events. If they coincided with a conjunction of the moon and Mars this would most plausibly result in an unfavorable astrological interpretation. A Late Babylonian practice of astrological historiography is clearly evident in BM 41222 (*ADRT* 5 52), another planetary excerpt with conjunctions, for example (side A col. ii 1'–6'):

> Year 14 of Šamaš-šum-ukin, Month XII, the 4th, Mercury's first appearance in the west in the area of the Swallow. When it became high, it was balanced 6 cubits above [Mar]s, Mercury .... [....]
> Year 17, Month II, the 19th, Mars was in [the area] of the Old Man to the right of Mercury 2 cu[bits ...]

---

3 The connections between the historical sections of the astronomical diaries and celestial omen divination were pointed out by Pirngruber 2013.

Year 19, Month VII, the 4th, Mercury stood for 2/3 cubit above Mars, Mercury [...]
Year 1 of Kandalānu, Month III, the 28th, Mercury was behind Mars ... [...] the 29th, it was 14 fingers above Mercury in the area of the Lion [....]

As argued elsewhere,[4] the author of this tablet selected conjunctions of Mercury and Mars to provide astrological context for a selection of significant events from the Babylonian past, such as rebellions and the death of kings, in an apparent effort to explain these events. Some of the underlying historical events are described in the Babylonian Chronicles, which were written by the same community of scholars as the astronomical diaries and related texts.[5] The conjunctions were either extracted from other astronomical diaries and related texts or, perhaps, retro-computed with the Goal Year method from more recent conjunctions, for instance with the help of the 32-year period mentioned on BM 76488. Mercury was conceived as a manifestation of Nabû, the Babylonian god of writing and accounting and a deity closely connected to kingship, while Mars was a malefic planet. Conjunctions between these planets were therefore most likely interpreted as unfavorable signs for the king. Planetary conjunctions continued to play an important role in later practices of astrological historiography. For instance, the Persian Jewish scholar Māshā'allāh (ca. 740–815 CE), a court astrologer in Abbasid Baghdad, developed a theory in which historical and political events are aligned with conjunctions of Jupiter and Saturn.[6] A dependence on Babylonian doctrines is difficult to establish, but cannot be excluded.

---

4 Ossendrijver and Waerzeggers 2025. For a discussion of the divinatory relevance of the content of the historical sections of the astronomical diaries see Pirngruber 2013.
5 For editions of the Babylonian Chronicles see Glassner 2004; van der Spek et al. 2025.
6 In his Arabic treatise *On Conjunctions, Religions, and Peoples*, which is partly preserved in quotations by the Christian astrologer Ibn Hibinta (Kennedy and Pingree 1971).

7 Babylonian evidence for cyclicity beyond astronomical phenomena

Babylonian scholars did not limit their efforts to develop predictive methods to celestial phenomena. They also investigated river levels, weather, market prices, and historical events—non-astronomical phenomena with complex and less obviously predictable patterns of temporal variability—and developed cycle-based methods for predicting them. The astronomical diaries and related texts can be viewed as products of these investigations, because they systematically report weather phenomena, river levels, market prices, and historical events alongside the astronomical phenomena, although without any explicit indication as to why this is done. The methods for predicting weather phenomena and market rates are attested in several procedure texts. The nature and the terminology of these procedures confirm that they were developed by scholars deeply familiar with the astronomical diaries and related texts, Goal Year methods, and the omen tradition.

7.1 Non-astronomical phenomena in the astronomical diaries and related texts

The astronomical diaries and related texts are conventionally referred to as genres of Babylonian astronomy, but this is in fact inaccurate. In addition to the lunar, planetary, solar, and other astronomical phenomena described in Section 4.1, weather phenomena are reported together with the astronomical phenomena, while market rates, the level of the river Euphrates, and local and political events in the city of Babylon occupy separate paragraphs in each monthly section.[1] The scope of the reported phenomena thus ranges from celestial and terrestrial natural phenomena to economic and political phenomena. Perhaps the only common feature of the reported phenomena is that they, at least from the Babylonian divinatory point of view, are communal and universal phenomena in the sense that they can be perceived by or affect the community as a whole.

The market rates of the following six important agricultural staple are reported: barley, dates, *kasû* (cuscuta?), sesame, *saḫlû* (a type of cress), and wool. The values of the market rates represent the amounts that could be acquired for 1

---

[1] For a discussion of the content and the structure of the historical sections of the astronomical diaries see Pirngruber 2013.

shekel of silver, so that they correspond to the inverse of a modern price. For barley, dates, *kasû*, *saḥlû* and sesame the market rate is expressed as a volume, for wool as a weight. Scholars agree that the reported rates are based on empirical data. For barley and dates the market rate was usually reported at the beginning, in the middle, and at the end of the month; for *kasû*, *saḥlû*, sesame, and wool once per month. The frequency of reporting may reflect specific assumptions about how the market rates are correlated with astronomical phenomena. A time resolution of one report per month reveals how market rates vary from month to month. A frequency of three reports per month reveals additional variations within each month. Perhaps these market rates were assumed to be correlated with Lunar Six intervals, which are similarly distributed over the beginning, the middle and the end of the month. This is supported by *ADRT* 5 43, an undated tablet from Babylon with Lunar Six data and market rates. Further evidence for Babylonian efforts to establish regularities in market rates are the commodity price lists, a small corpus of about 17 Late Babylonian tablets from Babylon.[2] They contain values of the market rate for one commodity for periods ranging from one year to dozens of years which were probably compiled with the aim of revealing long-term trends.

The reported weather phenomena include several types of rain, hail, dew, mist, several types of cloud, lightning, thunder, rainbows, halos, several types of wind, and coldness. The terminology used for reporting weather phenomena is highly technical, not fully understood, and to a large extent unique to the astronomical diaries and related texts. The only weather-related phenomenon for which quantitative measures were reported is the level of the river Euphrates. Until ca. 350 BCE the change of river level was reported among the celestial phenomena, in later diaries it was reported in a separate paragraph after the market rates and before the historical section. After ca. 300 BCE the value of the river level, measured downward from a reference height, was reported once per month at the end of each monthly section. An indication that the scholars assumed the river level to be correlated with cyclical astronomical phenomena are lunar and solar eclipses, which sometimes triggered almost daily reporting of the river level. This is attested for observed eclipses and also for predicted eclipses that did not materialize. The frequent reporting usually sets in at least several days before the eclipse and it continues for several days after the eclipse. About a dozen examples of this practice are attested between 347 BCE and 88 BCE.[3] A similar intensification of reporting near eclipses applies to the market rates.[4]

---

2 Slotsky and Wallenfels 2009.
3 Ossendrijver 2021a, 247.

The systematic recording of non-astronomical and astronomical phenomena over six centuries strongly suggests an underlying assumption that the former are in some fashion related to the latter and that this may render them predictable. As explained in Section 4.2, most of the planetary and lunar phenomena reported in the astronomical diaries were in fact predictable by 600 BCE. This suggests that the method by which the non-astronomical phenomena were meant to be predicted is based on assumed correlations with cyclical astronomical phenomena. This is confirmed by the procedure texts which are discussed in the next section. It will also be argued that the Babylonian approach to the prediction of non-astronomical phenomena led to fundamental changes in the conceptualization of time and cyclicity that have not been fully recognized in previous scholarship on the Mesopotamian conceptions of time.

7.2 Procedures for predicting market rates and weather phenomena

The most explicit evidence for developments in the Babylonian methods for predicting non-astronomical phenomena by means of cycles is offered by the small corpus of Late Babylonian compendia with procedures for predicting market rates and weather phenomena.[5] The procedures can be divided into two distinct groups: 1) rules for long-term prediction, either formulated as a list of planetary periods embedded in general instructions, or as what will be referred to as recurrence rules; 2) inferential rules by which non-astronomical phenomena are predicted from astronomical phenomena. The long-term prediction of non-astronomical phenomena is achieved by combining both types of rules. This constitutes a major innovation with respect to the predictive methods known from the celestial omen series *Enūma Anu Enlil* and other divinatory texts. These earlier texts only contain predictions of weather phenomena and market developments from the second group. What is lacking is any reference to long-term predictability through the astronomical phenomena that feature as signifying configurations.

Our exploration of the Late Babylonian procedures for predicting weather and market rates sets out with the long-term procedures, which are usually written at the beginning of the compendia. The following example is found on *SpTU* 1 94, a tablet from Seleucid Uruk (obv. 1–4):

---

4 Ossendrijver 2019, 63–64.
5 Schreiber 2018; Ossendrijver 2019; Ossendrijver 2021a.

7.2 Procedures for predicting market rates and weather phenomena — 45

> If you want to make a prediction for the region of the market rate of barley: broken — you investigate the course of the planets and you observe the (first) appearance, the last appearance, the station, the "balancing", the approaching, the faintness and brightness of the planets, and the zodiacal sign in which they begin to ascend and descend, and then you make a prediction for your year, and it will be correct.

We learn that in order to predict the market rate of barley—one of the commodities reported in the astronomical diaries—various phenomena of the planets must be investigated and that this will make it possible to predict the market rate for a future year. The precise method is not specified, but the reference to observation and the expression "your year", familiar from the Goal Year procedures, suggest that the Goal Year method is one component of the predictive method. This is confirmed by several long-term procedures for the prediction of weather by means of Goal Year periods, for instance (AO 6488 rev. 1–4; AO 6455 rev. 23):[6]

> [If] you (want to) cast a prediction [for rain and] high water: you [...] ....
> For Jupiter 1,12 (= 72), 24, 12 years; [for Venus] 16, 8 years; for Mercury 46, 21, 13 years; [for Saturn ... for Mars] 47 years; for the sun 36, 54 years; for the Moon 18 years.
> In order for you to compute rain and high water: 1,12 for Jupiter, 64, secondly 16 for Venus, 46, secondly 13 for Mercury, 59 for Saturn, 1,19 (= 79), secondly 47 for Mars.

A comparison with Table 3 reveals that some of these periods are standard Goal Year periods for predicting Normal Star passages and synodic phenomena of the planets. Most of the other periods (e.g. 12 years for Jupiter) are valid alternative Goal Year periods.[7] Rules of this kind are completely unknown from earlier compositions with weather predictions such as the omen series *Enūma Anu Enlil*. Even though knowledge of certain planetary periods, in particular the 8-year period for Venus, is implicit in the omen texts, as explained above, there is no evidence that they were combined with the omen statements to infer long-term weather predictions from the phenomena of Venus or any other planet.[8]

Additional clues about the use of planetary phenomena for long-term prediction are offered by so-called recurrence statements, which establish links between past and future occurrences of weather phenomena, or between past and future co-occurrences of astronomical and weather phenomena (AO 6488 rev. 5–13, 15–16). Some of them use the template "As much as previously W, now W", where W is a weather phenomenon, for example (rev. 6a, 7b):

---

6 For editions of these texts see Hunger 1976; Brack-Bernsen and Hunger 2002.
7 Ossendrijver 2021a, 230.
8 On this topic see also Brown 2000, 3, 193–207.

> [As much as] there were clouds before, there will be clouds now. (...)
> As much as there was "loosening of the sandal" before, there will be "loosening of the sandal" now.

It is highly significant that many of the weather terms mentioned in these statements belong to the technical terminology of the astronomical diaries and related texts and are not attested elsewhere. One example of such a term is the "loosening of the sandal", which is often reported in the astronomical diaries and most likely denotes some intensity of rain. This is a clear indication that the weather procedures were formulated by scholars deeply familiar with the astronomical diaries. It confirms that at least some scholars connected to the diary project pursued the development of methods for predicting non-astronomical phenomena, as was proposed above. Other recurrence statements in the same text are more explicit about the role of planetary phenomena as predictable signifiers of weather phenomena (AO 6488 rev. 10–13, 15–16):

> [If] the planets appear and there is rain and high water, now rain and high water.
> If on the 2nd day after its appearance rain and high water then now on the 2nd day after its appearance rain and high water.
> [If on the 3]rd rain and high water then now the same.
> If on the 4th rain and high water then now the same.

In other words, if the weather phenomenon rain and high water (presumably of a specific intensity or quality) once coincided with the first appearance of a planet, then the same weather phenomenon will repeat in the future whenever the planetary phenomenon occurs again, with the same delay between them as before. The intervals between "before" and "now" are not specified, but the position of the recurrence statements immediately after the list of planetary Goal Year periods (rev. 1–4) strongly suggests that they constitute the time intervals between "before" and "now", consistent with the mention of the signifying planetary phenomena. It can be assumed that these recurrence statements are expressions of a more general rule, namely that the time delay between the signifying planetary phenomenon, i.e. not only first appearances, and the associated weather phenomenon, i.e. not only rain and high water, is the same for past and future instances of the planetary phenomenon. AO 6488 ends with certain intercalation rules (rev. 18–19) which are needed for determining the "new month" when the Goal Year period is added to the "old month".[9] This adds further plausibility to the conclusion that the weather predictions are meant to be obtained with Goal

---

9 Hunger 1976b, 246.

7.2 Procedures for predicting market rates and weather phenomena — 47

Year periods, because they correspond to fixed numbers of months and corrections expressed in days, as explained above.

Most of the remaining procedures for predicting weather and market rates are inferential statements by which developments in weather or market rates are inferred from signifying configurations involving planets or the moon. Apart from omen statements of the conventional form "If P then Q", some inferential statements in these compendia use other prepositions than the conditional if, for instance "as soon as" or "when".[10] As discussed elsewhere,[11] the signifying configurations that appear in these texts form three categories. First, zodiacal signs or constellations without reference to planets; secondly, single planets or the moon; thirdly, conjunctions, oppositions and other simultaneous phenomena of two planets. The following examples belong to the second kind (*SpTU* 1 94 obv. 5–8):

> Normally Jupiter in the Lion (Leo), Pabilsag (Sagittarius), between the Goat-Fish (Capricorn) and the Great One (Aquarius) and the region of the Bristle (Pleiades) and the Bull of Heaven (Taurus): the market rate will increase and in all (other) zodiacal signs the market rate will decrease. And Saturn from the Crab (Cancer) until Pabilsag (Sagittarius): it will increase; from the Goat-Fish (Capricorn) until the Great Twins (Gemini): it will decrease.

In these statements market developments are inferred from the positions of individual planets.[12] It can be assumed that the inferences are immediate, because no delay is specified between the occurrence of the planetary configuration and the onset of the weather phenomenon or market development signified by it. Recall that the market rate is the amount of a commodity that could be acquired for a fixed amount of silver, so that it corresponds to the inverse of a modern price. In the Mesopotamian context a high market rate counted as a favorable thing, a low market rate as an unfavorable thing.[13] Similar inferential rules involving single planets and specific locations in the zodiac exist for weather prediction (AO 6449 obv. 21–23):

> When a planet appears in the region of rain: it will rain that day; until it emerges from it, the clouds will not be cut off: it is because clouds and rain correspond.

---

10 For a discussion of the Mesopotamian approach to inference from signs see Rochberg 2010.
11 Ossendrijver 2021a, 233–242.
12 The fact that the Bristle and the Bull of Heaven are mentioned, constellations in the zodiacal sign Taurus, could indicate that the spatial framework underlying this passage is not that of the uniform zodiac, but that of Normal Stars and constellations. However, other procedures on the tablet do employ the uniform zodiac. It is therefore plausible that the combination "Bristle and Bull of Heaven" designates the zodiacal sign Taurus.
13 Ossendrijver 2019, 54.

The full extent of the "region of rain" is unknown, but the Crab (Cancer), the Lion (Leo), the Great One (Aquarius), and the Tails (Pisces) were probably part of it, either as constellations or as zodiacal signs.[14] Hence the long-term prediction of rain boils down to the prediction of a planet's first appearance in specific zodiacal regions, which can be achieved with Goal Year methods.

The most commonly used signifying configurations in these procedures are conjunctions, oppositions, and other phenomena involving two planets. This constitutes a significant departure from earlier omen texts, in which non-astronomical phenomena were predominantly predicted from single planets. The following quotation covers conjunctions and oppositions of Jupiter and Saturn (AO 6449 obv. 32–37):

> Passings, which Jupiter and Saturn perform together: for 2 days, 3 days abundant rain and high water. At the opposition, when Jupiter stands in the Lion (Leo) and Saturn in the Great One (Aquarius), rain and high water for the lands you predict, a rise of the market rate, prospering of Nisaba you predict. When they stand together in the Great One or the Lion, rain and high water, a rise of the market rate you predict.

The procedures include numerous similar rules involving conjunctions and oppositions between Jupiter and Mars, Jupiter and Mercury, Saturn and Venus, Mercury and Mars, Mercury and Saturn, and Venus and Mercury. They illustrate that predictions of weather and market rates are usually inferred from conjunctions or oppositions involving one benefic or ambiguous planet (Venus, Jupiter, Mercury) and one malefic or ambiguous planet (Mars, Saturn, Mercury). This appears to be a general principle, but we can only speculate about the underlying reasoning. Perhaps it reflects the inherently ambiguous nature of weather, which is a condition for human existence, but can also destroy it. The following examples cover conjunctions of Venus and Mercury, including a near conjunction of these planets with Jupiter (AO 6449 rev. 25–30):

> Passings, which Venus and Mercury perform together. Whether in a high position or in a low position: rain and flood, you evaluate the positions. (If) Mercury is high behind Venus in the Lion (Leo) in the west, or approaches (it) and becomes stationary behind Venus: much rain, Tigris and Euphrates will carry their flood. When Jupiter stands in front of the King star (Regulus): you predict rain and flood when Venus and Mercury pass by this constellation.

The instruction to "evaluate the positions" is repeatedly found in these procedures. It implies that the predictions are affected by the zodiacal signs in which the planets are located. The following example introduces planetary brightness

---

14 Ossendrijver 2021a, 238.

and faintness as additional factors that can affect market rates (*SpTU* I 94, obv. 12–14):

> If Jupiter is faint or it takes up a low position or it disappears (after its last appearance) and Mars is bright or takes up a high position or Mars is 'balanced' (in conjunction) with Jupiter: the market rate will strongly decrease and the people will experience a large famine.

This is one of many instances where we can identify analogical reasoning in the connections that are established between planetary and terrestrial phenomena. Since Jupiter is a benefic planet, its faintness or low position (presumably with respect to the ecliptic) signifies negative developments, as does the brightness or the high position of the malefic planet Mars. However, the inclusion of planetary brightness and faintness as co-determining factors complicates the long-term predictability of market rates from planetary phenomena, because there is no conclusive textual evidence that Babylonian scholars had developed methods for predicting brightness and faintness.[15] As far as currently known, the brightness or faintness of a planet could only be established through observation, in which case this inferential rule could not be used for long-term prediction.

The predictive method that emerges from the long-term procedures and the inferential rules comprises two stages: long-term prediction of planetary phenomena using Goal Year-type methods and short-term inference of weather and market phenomena from the planetary phenomena thus predicted. Each of these stages corresponds to a different approach to prediction: a period-based approach for the planetary phenomena and an inferential approach rooted in celestial divination for weather and market phenomena. The quoted procedures indicate that the long-term prediction of planetary phenomena was meant to be achieved with the Goal Year method. In principle the same could be achieved with the methods of mathematical astronomy, which result in tables of synodic phenomena and daily positions covering much longer intervals of time than possible with the Goal Year method. But there is no concrete evidence that the inferential rules were combined with mathematical astronomy to produce very long-term predictions of weather or market rates.

The question of the practical use of the procedures also remains unanswered. Recall that the methods for predicting lunar and planetary phenomena (Goal Year method, mathematical astronomy) are attested both in procedure texts and in the form of concrete predictions for future years (Goal Year Texts, Almanacs, Normal Star Almanacs, synodic tables and daily motion tables). By contrast, the methods

---

[15] Possible references to brightness and faintness as a predictable quantity occur on the Late Babylonian astrological tablet BM 32339+32407+32645 (Ossendrijver 2018b).

for predicting weather and market rates are only attested in procedure texts, while there is no textual evidence for actual predictions of market rates and weather phenomena for concrete future dates. This raises doubts about the predictive use of these procedures. Even though they are predictive rules in a formal sense, it seems possible that they served a different purpose than prediction, namely to "explain" past developments in weather and market rates recorded in diaries and chronicles in the sense of identifying the astronomical phenomena that announced these developments.[16] Concrete evidence for the use of predictive astronomy for explaining the past is presented in Section 6.2.

7.3 Evidence for intrinsic cyclicity of non-astronomical phenomena

In the procedure texts discussed above, long-term prediction of weather phenomena and market rates is achieved by means of cycle-based methods for predicting astronomical phenomena that act as their signifying configurations. Even though the recurrence statements are explicit about the cyclical repetition of weather phenomena, the procedures maintain a subtle distinction between the cyclicity of planetary phenomena, which is presented as an intrinsic feature, and the cyclicity of non-astronomical phenomena, which is not presented as intrinsic but as imparted by the associated planetary phenomena. However, some Late Babylonian astrological texts contain statements that do appear to assign intrinsic cyclicity to non-astronomical phenomena, without any indication that these periods are imparted by planets or the moon. The following examples occur in a compendium of Goal Year procedures and astrological procedures from Uruk written near 200 BCE (AO 6455 rev. 28):[17]

> In 21 years rain will correspond to rain, high water to high water.
> In 21 years an earthquake will correspond to an earthquake.
> In 6 hundred 54 years – broken.

The 21-year period for rain, high water, and earthquakes is presented as an intrinsic period without any connection to planets. Indeed the 21-year period is not attested elsewhere in connection with planetary phenomena. The passage about the period of 654 years was damaged on the original which the scribe was copying. It

---

16 See Ossendrijver 2021a.
17 At least partly duplicated in BM 37056+37074, an unpublished Late Babylonian astrological compendium from Babylon (edition by John Steele forthcoming).

might pertain to a non-astronomical phenomenon, but this is very uncertain.[18] Another potentially intrinsic cycle of rain and high water mentioned on the tablet is equally difficult to interpret (AO 6455 rev. 24):

> In order for you to compute rain and high water: (...) you turn back behind you 9 UŠ ŠAR$_2$ ŠAR$_2$ ŠAR$_2$ ŠAR$_2$ ŠAR$_2$ ŠAR$_2$ ŠAR$_2$ ŠAR$_2$ ŠAR$_2$ (years) and you ...

The interpretation of this confusing numerical expression, which contains an unusual combination of elements of an ancient Mesopotamian number notation, is open to debate. Perhaps it represents 9 x 60 + 9 x 3600 = 32,940 years or 9 x 60 x 9 x 3600 = 17,496,000 years.[19] Since this period is not attributed to a planet, it appears to be conceived of as an intrinsic cycle of rain and high water. Its origin is fully unclear. Since the scribe copied the tablet from a damaged original, as indicated by several glosses "broken", and no parallels are known, he may have had difficulty in understanding the content. However, these periods are at least vaguely reminiscent of the Greco-Roman Great Years.[20]

7.4 Babylonian horoscopes

Horoscopy emerged in Babylonia as a new astrological practice in the wake of the introduction of the uniform zodiac near the end of the fifth century BCE. The practice of horoscopy reflects a "personal turn" in astrology, because horoscopes are concerned with private individuals, unlike earlier forms of Mesopotamian celestial divination, which only served kings. Horoscopy spread from Babylonia to Greco-Roman Egypt and beyond after the second century BCE (Section 11.1). Most Babylonian horoscopes report nothing more than the positions of the moon, the sun, and the five planets in the zodiacal signs.[21] It is only rarely the case that predictions for the newborn were added; that information was usually communicated orally by the astrologer. It is also important to stress that horoscopes are entirely the result of computation. First, they were often produced many years after the birth of the child; secondly, the seven bodies are never simultaneously visible on a

---

18 Gysembergh 2023 points out that some Byzantine and Greco-Roman sources connect this period with the appearance of the phoenix, a mythological bird.
19 In the traditional Mesopotamian number notation UŠ stands for 60 and ŠAR$_2$ for 3600. The tentative interpretations offered here assume that 9 UŠ = 9 x 60 and each instance of ŠAR$_2$ stands for 3600.
20 See Brown 2018, 401.
21 For an edition of the Babylonian horoscopes see Rochberg 1998. See also Rochberg 2004, 121–208; Pilloni 2024.

given date and the zodiacal position of the sun is not accessible through observation; thirdly, positions are always expressed in the zodiacal framework typical for mathematical astronomy, whereas zodiacal signs are not observable. It follows that the practice of horoscopy relies on access to tables of planetary positions computed with mathematical astronomy and that the dissemination of horoscopy through the ancient world necessarily overlaps with the dissemination of mathematical astronomy.

Since the computational techniques of mathematical astronomy are based on models of cyclical motion, horoscopes are, strictly speaking, also cyclical. The configuration will repeat whenever the seven wandering bodies return to the same zodiacal positions. One might be tempted to conclude from this that inferences drawn from such horoscopes should also be identical, which would impart a notion of cyclicity to human fate. No such conclusion is mentioned or implied in any Babylonian text and it seems doubtful that a Babylonian astrologer would accept it.

7.5 Schematic luni-solar cycles in microzodiac texts and calendar texts

The introduction of the zodiac also triggered developments in astrological medicine. In this context Babylonian scholars developed a sophisticated spatial-temporal framework for organizing and formulating astrological doctrines, which is based on the zodiac and the schematic calendar.[22] Within this spatial-temporal framework they constructed two elementary numerical schemes for the motion of the moon and sun that came to play a central role in astro-medical and divinatory practices. The conceptual building blocks of the schemes are 1) a uniform zodiac with 12 signs of 30°, 2) a schematic year with 12 synodic months of 30 days, 3) a daily solar motion along the zodiac of 1°, and 4) a daily lunar motion along the zodiac of 13°. Under these assumptions the sun carries out one complete cycle around the zodiac in one year, starting in 13 Aries on Day 1 of Month I, and there is a one-to-one correspondence between dates and degree positions in the zodiac. The moon moves 13 times faster than the sun, proceeding by 30 x 13 = 390° per month, corresponding to one full revolution around the zodiac plus 30°. The sun covers 30° in this interval, so that it will again be in conjunction with the moon. Two interrelated numerical schemes were constructed from these elements, known in modern scholarship as the Dodecatemoria scheme

---

22 See also Koch 2016, 213–216.

7.5 Schematic luni-solar cycles in microzodiac texts and calendar texts

and the Calendar Text scheme. Both schemes assume the form of a table of 360 entries, one for every day of the schematic calendar or degree of the zodiac. The first 14 entries of both schemes are as follows (Tab. 5):

Tab. 5: Schematic luni-solar cycles of the Dodecatemoria scheme and the Calendar Text scheme

Dodecatemoria scheme				Calendar Text scheme			
month	day	sign	degree	month	day	sign	degree
1	1	1	13	1	1	10	7
1	2	1	26	1	2	7	14
1	3	2	9	1	3	4	21
1	4	2	22	1	4	1	28
1	5	3	5	1	5	11	5
1	6	3	18	1	6	8	12
1	7	4	1	1	7	5	19
1	8	4	14	1	8	2	26
1	9	4	27	1	9	12	3
1	10	5	10	1	10	9	10
1	11	5	23	1	11	6	17
1	12	6	6	1	12	3	24
1	13	6	19	1	13	1	1
1	14	7	2	1	14	10	8
etc.				etc.			

In both schemes the numbers in columns 1 and 3 are between 1 and 12, while those in columns 2 and 4 are between 1 and 30. The astronomical meaning of the Dodecatemoria scheme is intuitively clear: the first pair expresses a date, the second pair the corresponding position of the moon, which is in 13 Aries on Day 1 of Month I (or in 30 Pisces on Day 30 of Month XII). In the Calendar Text scheme the longitudes proceed by 9 zodiacal signs and 7°, i.e. 277°, from day to day. The ingenious origin of this seemingly arbitrary number was clarified by Lis Brack-Bernsen and John Steele.[23] The Calendar Text scheme is not independent from the Dodecatemoria scheme, but was obtained from it through a sequence of manipulations, namely exchanging columns 1–2 (dates) and columns 3–4 (positions), reinterpreting the positions as dates and vice versa, and rearranging the entries strictly by date. For example, the entry 1 1 1 13 became 1 13 1 1, which was assigned to Month I Day 13 in the Calendar Text scheme. The apparent daily progression of 277° is merely a consequence of these manipulations. Note

---

[23] Brack-Bernsen and Steele 2004.

that the interpretation of schematic dates (month, day) as positions in the zodiac (sign, degree) and vice versa is very common in Late Babylonian astrology. The spatial-temporal ambiguity of the astrological number schemes is strengthened by the numerical identity of the dates and the positions of the sun for these dates. In many astrological contexts, numbers 1–12 can be interpreted either as months of the schematic calendar or as zodiacal signs, and analogously numbers 1–30 can be interpreted either as days of the schematic month or as degrees.

The mentioned schemes are mainly known from their application in microzodiac texts, Calendar Texts, and other astro-medical texts. These Late Babylonian genres testify to fundamental changes in astrological, divinatory, and healing practices. Calendar Texts form a series of twelve tablets, one for every zodiacal sign and the corresponding month. Each tablet provides medical ingredients, cultic, and hemerological instructions for one month of the schematic calendar and the corresponding zodiacal sign. This is exemplified by the following entry from the Calendar Text for Month I (Aries), which pertains to Day 7:

5 19 1 7
Šiqdu wood, azallû plant, anzaḫḫu stone. Nippur – Ekur. Day of the citygod Šamaš, judge of the land, and of the hero Šulpaea: opening of the gate. He should libate water for the Anunnaki, pray to Enlil. A legal case: not favorable. He should not look at a snake. 4 1.

The numbers 5 19 1 7 constitute Entry 7 from the Calendar Text scheme, except that the columns are switched for some unknown reason. They are followed by an entry from the so-called Stone-Plant-Wood Scheme, various cultic and hemerological instructions and, at the end, numbers from the Dodecatemoria scheme (4 1) for the same day (1 7). A subset of the data contained in Calendar Texts is also found on the microzodiac tablets, but arranged differently. They also form a series of 12 tablets, one for each zodiacal sign and the corresponding month of the schematic calendar. On these tablets each zodiacal sign is subdivided into 12 microzodiac signs starting with the first microsign which is named after the main sign, i.e. in the case of Aries from Aries of Aries to Pisces of Aries. On the microzodiac tablet for Leo / Month V we find the same entry "Šiqdu wood, azallû plant, anzaḫḫu stone" from the Stone-Plant-Wood Scheme assigned to Aries of Leo, the ninth microsign of Leo, where Leo corresponds to the 5 in 5 19 1 7, and Aries corresponds to the 1 in that sequence. Analogous numerical correspondences apply between all other entries of the Calendar Texts and microzodiac texts.

Even though many practical details about the use of the Calendar Texts and the microzodiac texts remain unclear, it is apparent that certain medical procedures and aspects of daily life were determined by looking up the appropriate entries in these texts, setting out from a date and/or a zodiacal position. The latter practice has a precursor in pre-zodiacal hemerologies, which list propitiousness or non-propitiousness for the days and months of the year.[24] Since the numerical schemes underlying the calendar texts and microzodiac texts derive from schematic models of solar and lunar motion through the zodiac, this points to new roles for the moon and the sun as agents that signify or determine, astrological, medical, and divinatory practices, and human life in general. The texts are silent about the reasons why these doctrines are built upon the schematic motion of the moon and the sun, but we may speculate that this developed out of their fundamental role in the luni-solar calendar and, perhaps, because more than the five planets, the two luminaries, i.e. the Sungod and the Moongod, obviously shape daily life through the variations which they produce in their fundamental cycles, the year, and the month.

7.6 Hidden agency of the planets in Late Babylonian astrology

As indicated by the cuneiform sources discussed above, Late Babylonian scholars dedicated most of their attention to the Moon and the planets. In a parallel development, some Late Babylonian temple rituals invoke the planets directly instead of the major deities associated with them,[25] which indicates that they were granted a degree of agency. In order to obtain a broader understanding of the reasons why Late Babylonian scholars may have used planetary cycles for predicting non-astronomical phenomena, this section explores several Late Babylonian sources in which the hidden nature of planetary agency can be identified as a common thread. It will be argued that this notion can shed light on the use of planetary cycles in Late Babylonian predictive science.

The first source to be mentioned is the tablet 11N-T4, a learned medical commentary from Nippur in southern Babylonia with traces of a doctrine known as planetary melothesia.[26] According to this doctrine, which is also known from Greco-Roman astro-medicine, body parts are associated with planets. The complete set of associations (sun: heart/stomach; moon: liver; Jupiter: spleen; Mars, Venus: kidneys; Saturn, Mercury: lungs) was reconstructed by Marvin Schreiber.[27]

---

24 See Livingstone 2013.
25 See for instance Krul 2018, 181–190.
26 Editions: Civil 1974, 336–338; Frazer 2015; discussion: Reiner 1995, 59–60; Frahm 2011, 231–232; Schreiber 2022, 479–480.
27 Schreiber 2022, 479–480.

The following two statements from 11N-T4 deal with elements of this doctrine (obv. 6–7; 20–21):

> If a man's spleen hurts him: he should seek out the temple of Marduk and he will be cured. As it is said about this: ŠA₃.GIG ("sick interior") means Jupiter, ŠA₃.GIG means spleen. (…) If a man's kidney hurts him: hand of Nergal. As it is said, the Kidney Star is Mars.

The purpose of the tablet is to explain the connections between internal organs (spleen, kidney) and planets (Jupiter, Mars) by means of *tertia comparationis* rooted in scribal scholarship. The doctrine of planetary melothesia is premised on the existence of connections between planets and organs, which are hidden parts of the human body. In that regard it constitutes a clear contrast with the coexisting Babylonian doctrine of zodiacal melothesia, which associates the twelve zodiacal signs with visible parts of the human body from head to foot.[28]

The notion of hidden planetary agency may also underlie several statements about the origin of eclipses attested in Late Babylonian tablets from Babylon and Uruk.[29] The following example is preserved on SpTU 4 161, a tablet from Uruk dated to ca. 445–485 BCE (rev. 1–5):

> If an eclipse of (the Sungod) Šamaš is before you: the planet, which (the Moongod) Sîn passed (in) the month of your watch of Šamaš from <Day 16> until Day 28, it caused the eclipse of Šamaš to occur, that planet is the origin of its sign for the land.

A close duplicate is preserved on a tablet from Babylon. The statements are expressions of a theory of eclipse causation in which causative agency is, surprisingly, assigned to the planets. The cause of a solar eclipse is said to be that planet which the moon passes in the month of the eclipse between Day 16, near full moon, and Day 28, shortly before the eclipse. Since the moon travels almost half the zodiac in this period, it is virtually certain to pass by at least one planet. The statement quoted above mentions two complementary acts of causation: first, the planet causes the eclipse to happen; secondly, it provides the eclipse with a specific ominous significance for king and country. The precise manner in which the planets realize their agency in causing eclipses when the moon passes by remains unclear. One can only speculate about the underlying scenario; perhaps the idea is that the Moongod interacts with the planet in some fashion.

It is important to point out that this theory about the cause of eclipses did not interfere with the Babylonian methods for predicting eclipses. The saros-based

---

28 For the zodiacal melothesia in Babylonia see Wee 2015; Geller 2014; Schreiber 2022.
29 See Ossendrijver 2025.

method and the algorithms of mathematical astronomy are based on a detailed understanding of the cyclical motions of moon and sun and the conditions that must be satisfied during an eclipse. According to these methods, eclipses can happen if the oppositions and the conjunctions of the moon and the sun occur sufficiently close to the intersections of their celestial paths, with no consideration whatsoever for the planets. It follows that the agency of the planets in causing eclipses operates in a distinct manner isolated from the methods for eclipse prediction, so that we may indeed speak of hidden agency.

A third set of expressions that could reflect a notion of hidden planetary agency concerns so-called cryptographic omens, which are preserved on several Late Babylonian tablets from Babylon.[30] In these otherwise formally regular omens, the protases are written as sequences of numbers in sexagesimal place value notation, for example (BM 92685 obv. 9–13):

> 12 5 6 1 11.30 4 31: the furrow will prosper, the land of Elam will be destroyed, the king of the world [...]
> 12 5 6 1 7 4 31: the furrow will prosper, the land of Elam will be destroyed, the demise of Assur [...]
> 12 5 6 1 4 4 31: the furrow will decrease, later that year the market rate will flourish, in the land [...]
> 12 5 6 1 3 4 31: the furrow will decrease, later that year the market rate will flourish, in the land [...]

The numbers that constitute the protases do not belong to a well-known system of Babylonian cryptography. But based on the structure of the statements, Hermann Hunger was able to show that 12, 11.30, 7, 4, and 3 denote the planets Jupiter, Venus, Mercury, Saturn, and Mars, respectively, and that most of the omens deal with conjunctions between two planets—yet another piece of evidence for the important role of planetary conjunctions in predictive practices. The quoted omens cover conjunctions of Jupiter (12) with the other four planets. The third number probably denotes the zodiacal sign, i.e. Virgo (6), and the number 4 31 probably represents a verb for conjunction. It is probably significant that this cryptography is attested only in Late Babylonian omen texts about conjunctions. This can be interpreted as further support for the idea that planetary agency was considered to operate in a hidden fashion. The omens are followed by two partly preserved sections with statements about planets:[31]

---

30 Hunger 1969.
31 Hunger 1969, 141; Brown 2000, 193.

> Jupiter [to ...]
> Venus to [...]
> Mercury to [...]
> Saturn to [...]
> Mars to (the Moongod) Sin [...]
> ___
> He eclipsed 71 years.
> He laid waste 60 years.
> He established 59 years.
> He ordered 8 years.
> He prolonged 15 years.
> He rejoiced 12 years.

It is plausible that the first section contained predictions based on planets approaching the moon, consistent with the topic of conjunctions. The second section lists activities that are difficult to make sense of. They are implicitly ascribed to planets, because the statements mention Goal Year type periods of Jupiter (71 and 12 years), Saturn (59 years), Venus (8 years), Mars (15 years), and Mercury (60 years). It is therefore possible that these statements express ideas about planetary agency in the preceding omens, but the precise nature of the connection is difficult to determine.

Finally, the Late Babylonian astrological tablet BM 35402 (*LBAT* 1593) contains omens of a kind unknown from the series *Enūma Anu Enlil* in which the future of a newborn is inferred from planetary and lunar phenomena during birth.[32] The tablet concludes with an often-overlooked final section, which contains a list of planetary periods (rev. 12'–20'):[33]

> Long period of Jupiter: 3 hundred 44 years. Short period of Jupiter 1,3 (=63) months 10 days.
> Long period of Venus: 1,4 hundred (=6400) years. Short period of Venus 1,4 (=64) months 20 days.
> Short period of Venus: 7 days; for 14 days; for 21 days.
> Period of Mars: 1,5 (=65) months, for 6 months 20 days.
> Long period of Mars: for 284 years.
> [Period] of Saturn: for 10 months. Long period of Saturn: for 5 hundred (...) [...]
> Long [period] of the Moon: for 6 hundred 1,24 (=684) years.

---

32 Reiner 2000.
33 For editions of this section see Kugler 1907, 48–53, and the Electronic Babylonian Library website, https://www.ebl.lmu.de/library/BM.35402. The logographic expression UD.DA is translated provisionally as "period", based on the assumption that it is an abbreviation of UD.DA.ZAL.LA. By itself UD.DA means "glow", but this makes little sense and there is no known parallel for this usage of the word "glow".

The planets are listed in the usual Babylonian order from benefic to malefic, with the moon listed after the malefics. The period of 284 years for Mars is known from Babylonian mathematical astronomy (Section 5.1: Tab. 4). Interestingly, it is also mentioned by the Byzantine scholar John Lydus (fifth/sixth century CE) in the context of his computation of the Great Year.[34] The other periods are not attested in mathematical astronomy or in Goal Year methods. The question of why these periods are listed on a tablet with birth omens and what they were used for cannot be answered, even tentatively, for lack of context and cuneiform parallels. The syntax of the statements is also partly unclear. It seems possible that the periods are meant to be used for making predictions, presumably about the newborn.

---

34 See Section 11.2. I thank Levente László for pointing this out.

8 Towards a new understanding of the Late Babylonian conceptions of time and cyclicity

The preceding sections explored developments in Babylonian astral science affecting the knowledge of astronomical cycles, their conceptualization, and their use in predictive methods. With the onset of the astronomical diaries and the emergence of the Goal Year methods (ca. 600 BCE), Babylonian astronomy experienced a predictive turn. Henceforth most planetary and lunar phenomena were conceived of as periodic and fully predictable. A central role in the new predictive methods is played by the synodic cycle, which corresponds to a repetition of the relative spatial configuration of planet and sun. Goal Year periods contain multiple synodic cycles in order to achieve a close return in the spatial and temporal domains. In Goal Year procedures, past instances of astronomical phenomena are identified with future instances of the same phenomena separated by Goal Year periods. Predictability is therefore conceptualized in terms of periodic repetition, which amounts to a new understanding of predictability and periodicity. With the emergence of mathematical astronomy in the wake of the introduction of the uniform zodiac, the state of knowledge, the conceptualization, and the role of cyclicity as perceived by Babylonian scholars underwent further developments. The periods underlying mathematical astronomy are much longer than Goal Year periods and can exceed the entire timespan of the astronomical diaries. They are not tools of prediction, but properties of the algorithms. Even more so than with the Goal Year method, planetary and lunar phenomena are conceived of as instances of repeating sequences of such phenomena, that stretch from the distant past into the remote future.

In a related development, long-term predictive methods were developed for non-astronomical phenomena including weather, market rates, and possibly historical events. According to the extant procedure texts, two approaches to prediction are combined in these methods: one, long-term, cycle-based prediction of astronomical phenomena, and, two, inferential rules for predicting weather phenomena and market rates from more or less simultaneous astronomical phenomena. Prediction could be oriented towards the future, but also towards the past. By means of retro-computation, past events could be reconstructed or re-interpreted by identifying which astronomical phenomena had announced them. We can therefore speak of a conceptual shift in the Babylonian understanding of how time is structured, which took shape after ca. 600 BCE. In the new framework, astronomical phenomena, weather phenomena, and terrestrial phenomena are connected not only spatially in the vertical direction, but also horizontally through time. Past and future instances of these phenomena are tied together in repeating sequences, governed by planetary cycles. The most explicit textual evidence for the new framework are recurrence rules, which explicitly assert that the cyclical repetition of weather phenomena is imparted by the planets.

In this context, the topic of planetary conjunctions and oppositions rose to great prominence. This is reflected in the astronomical diaries and related texts, which include lists of reported conjunctions between planets, in a procedure text (BM 76488) listing Goal Year type periods for planetary conjunctions, and in procedure texts and tablets with omens and other inferential statements for predicting weather and terrestrial phenomena from planetary conjunctions and oppositions. However, no cuneiform evidence for an interest in conjunctions involving more than two planets has come to light. In particular, no precursor of the Greco-Roman doctrine of the Great Year, the period in which the conjunction of all planets signifies global destruction through fires or floods has been uncovered.

The evidence discussed above reveals that Babylonian scholars made increasing use of planetary agency in their efforts to explain and predict phenomena in different realms of existence. The precise nature of their agency—causal, communicative, or significatory—is often difficult to establish. It was argued that their agency was often perceived and represented as a hidden one that does not manifest itself directly to the untrained observer. This constitutes a contrast with the agency of the sun and the moon, whose cyclical effects on human existence are obvious to all. The effects of the planets are not immediately obvious, but they were evident to the Babylonian scholars who studied their phenomena, their periods, properties, and their correlations with non-astronomical phenomena. The prominent role assigned to planetary cycles amounts to a significant elaboration of the traditional luni-solar calendrical framework. On top of the elementary cycles of the sun and the moon which define the conventional division of time into days, months, and years, the new framework incorporates a multitude of planetary cycles, thereby creating correspondences and predictability across much longer intervals of time.

In order to obtain a better understanding of the new cyclical framework, it can be analyzed as a case of model-based knowledge production. This approach has been fruitfully applied to the computational methods of Babylonian mathematical astronomy and to iterative computations in Mesopotamian accounting.[1] The rarity of explicit evidence for language-based reasoning in Mesopotamian scholarly texts supports the idea that this approach can provide a more appropriate description of Babylonian scholarly practices. The Late Babylonian methods

---

1 See Rochberg 2018; Ossendrijver 2021b.

for predicting non-astronomical phenomena through their associations with predictable, cyclical planetary phenomena can, arguably, be regarded as simulations aimed at making sense of the world. The procedure texts and the inferential statements discussed above can be viewed as instructions for generating such simulations.

To conclude this section it is worthwhile to compare the Babylonian evidence for conceptions of cyclicity in astronomical and astrological sources with the following passage on the Chaldeans from the *Library of History* by Diodorus Siculus (ca. 50 BCE):[2]

> The Chaldeans say that the nature of the cosmos is eternal and neither had a coming-to-be from the beginning nor is going to obtain a passing-away later; that the arrangement and order of everything took place through a certain divine providence, and that now each of the things happening in the heavens is brought about not at random or spontaneously but by some defined and securely ratified judgement of the gods. Having made observations of the stars over many years, and found out the motions and powers of each of them most accurately of all people, they foretell to people many of the things that are going to happen. They say that the greatest contemplation and power pertains to the five stars called "wanderers", which they collectively name "interpreters" (*hermeneus*). They call them interpreters, because, whereas the other stars are nonwandering and having a single revolution with an orderly journey, these alone, making a journey each of its own, indicate the things that are going to happen, interpreting for people the intention of the gods. They say that they signify, to those who have chosen to pay accurate attention, some things by their rising, some by their setting, and some by their color. For (they say that) they sometimes show the magnitudes of the winds, sometimes the excesses of rainstorms or heat waves, and sometimes the risings of comets, and also eclipses of Sun and Moon, and earthquakes, and in a word all the circumstances arising from the environment, being beneficial and harmful not only to peoples and places but also to kings and random individuals.

The account agrees in many points with the Babylonian sources.[3] According to Diodorus the Chaldeans believed that the world is eternal and that the celestial phenomena are caused by deities, which is consistent with the Babylonian epic of creation. Unlike some other Greco-Roman scholars to be discussed below, Diodorus does not attribute the notion of a Great Year or a periodic destruction to the Chaldeans, consistent with their absence from the extant Babylonian sources. Most interesting is his assertion that the Chaldeans considered the five planets and their phenomena to be of utmost significance for predicting future events such as wind, rain, heat, comets, eclipses, earthquakes, and the fate of kings and private individuals. Methods for predicting winds, rain, and heat from planetary phenomena are

---

2 *Library of History* II 30–31 (Jones and Steele 2018).
3 See also Jones and Steele 2018, 343–346.

indeed attested in Late Babylonian predictive texts. Moreover, some tablets contain traces of a theory that eclipses are caused by planets (Section 7.6). However, the name "interpreters", which is what the Chaldeans called the planets according to Diodorus, has no known parallel in the Babylonian sources.

9 Cyclicity and cycle-based conceptions of time according to Plato and Aristotle

In this chapter the exploration of cyclicity moves to ancient Greece and the Greco-Roman world. While the previous chapter had to proceed mainly from primary sources, the present one can exploit a large body of research on conceptions of time and cyclicity in the classical sources. Major examples of this kind are de Callataÿ 1996 and Wolkenhauer 2011. However, some important primary sources, such as the Keskintos inscription and the Antikythera mechanism, have been largely ignored in scholarship on Greco-Roman conceptions of time. The focus of the chapter is on temporal cyclicity and not on more general conceptions of time. The difficult topic of a transfer of knowledge and concepts between Babylonia and the Greco-Roman world is occasionally addressed, taking into account the latest insights about cyclicity in Late Babylonian scholarship.[1]

9.1 Cyclicity and the Great Year according to Plato

Plato (427–347 BCE) is one of the earliest ancient Greek thinkers to have written extensively about astronomical cycles and their relation to time. His rather specific views on these matters have been very influential in the Greco-Roman world and beyond. The most relevant statements can be found in the *Timaeus* (ca. 360 BCE), where Plato lets the philosopher Timaeus explain how the Demiurge created the world.[2] The following passage establishes, in a nutshell, the connection between the planets and time (*Timaeus* 38c):

> The sun and moon and five other stars, which are called the planets, were created by him [the Demiurge] in order to distinguish and preserve the numbers of time; and when he had made their several bodies, he placed them in the orbits in which the circle of the Other was revolving, in seven orbits seven stars.

We learn that the Demiurge created the sun and the moon and the five planets in order to mark time and its divisions. They were put in orbits along the circle of the Other, Plato's term for the ecliptic, which is inclined to the circle of the Same, his

---

[1] I thank Levente László and Michael Zellmann-Rohrer for providing many corrections and useful suggestions for Chapters 9–11.
[2] For investigations of these passages see von Fritz 1971, 172–173; Gloy 1986; de Callataÿ 1996, 1–15; Böhme 1996; Mesch 2003; Schäfer 2005; Mesch 2009; Wolkenhauer 2011, 25–27; Bodnár 2021.

ə Open Access. © 2025 the author(s), published by De Gruyter. This work is licensed under the Creative Commons Attribution-NonCommercial-NoDerivatives 4.0 International License.
https://doi.org/10.1515/9783112224250-010

term for the celestial equator. Not much attention has been paid in scholarship to the non-trivial statement that the function of indicating time is not limited to the sun and the moon, but is also assigned to the five planets. This constitutes a point of agreement with the Late Babylonian cyclical framework discussed above, with its multitude of planetary periods superimposed on the elementary calendrical cycles of sun and moon. It is impossible to ascertain whether this reflects a transfer of knowledge from Babylonia, a case of inspiration by hearsay about Babylonian astral science, or a completely independent development, but the latter option seems rather unlikely for 360 BCE.[3] The second passage to be discussed provides more details about the role of the planets and it introduces the influential notion of the Perfect Year (*Timaeus* 39c):

> That there might be some visible measure of their relative swiftness and slowness as they proceeded in their eight courses, God lighted a fire, which we now call the sun, in the second from the earth of these orbits, that it might give light to the whole of heaven, and that the animals, as many as nature intended, might participate in number, learning arithmetic from the revolution of the Same and the Like. In this manner and for this reason night and day were created, being the period of the one most intelligent revolution. And the month is accomplished when the moon has completed her orbit and overtaken the sun, and the year when the sun has completed his own orbit. The periods of the rest have not been observed by men, save for a few; and men have no names for them, nor do they measure one against another by numerical reckoning, so that they barely know that the wanderings of these others are time at all, bewildering as they are in number and of surprisingly intricate pattern. None the less it is possible to grasp that the Perfect Number of time fulfils the Perfect Year at the moment when the relative speeds of all the eight revolutions have accomplished their courses together and reached their consummation, as measured by the circle of the uniformly moving Same.

Plato defines the periods of the planets in terms of the repetition of their (apparent) velocity and not their position, a detail that is often overlooked. The eighth course pertains to the daily motion of the sky along the circle of the Same. It is included in the argument, even though its velocity does not vary. In Plato's understanding, the period of a planet is the time in which it proceeds through a complete cycle of the variations of its velocity, for instance from the station, when it comes to a standstill and begins to move in the retrograde direction, until the next instance of that station. In other words, the fundamental period of planetary motion is for Plato the synodic cycle, as it is in Babylonian astronomy. From the cyclical nature of planetary motion he infers the existence of a Perfect Number and a corresponding Perfect Year, after which the velocity of all planets repeats itself. That is, the Perfect Number contains a whole number of synodic periods

---

[3] See Gysembergh 2013, 118–119.

of each planet. But how to measure these periods? According to Plato, humans learned arithmetic by counting the daily revolutions of the sun and the moon along the circle of the Same. Their fundamental cycles—days, months, and years—constitute the units in which other periods can be expressed. Even though Plato considers the planets to be predictable on account of the cyclical nature of their motion, this predictability is only a potential one, because the periods of the planets are unknown. This lack of knowledge also prevents the computation of the Perfect Number. If Plato had access to Babylonian periods, he could have proceeded as follows. The most common Babylonian values of the synodic periods of Venus and Mars are 8/5 years and 79/37 years, respectively (Table 3). The corresponding Perfect Year, taking into account only these two planets, is 8 × 79 = 632 years, which contains 5 × 79 = 395 synodic periods of Venus or 37 × 8 = 296 synodic periods of Mars. If more planets are included, the Perfect Year rapidly grows in length and the same happens if more accurate periods are used, such as 1151/720 years for Venus, a value attested in Babylonian mathematical astronomy (Section 5.1: Tab. 4).

Since the synodic cycle achieves a repetition of the relative spatial arrangement of planet and sun, the same is true for the Perfect Year. Only if the Perfect Year equals a whole number of solar years, as in the example, will the planets return to the same absolute position with respect to the stars.[4] Also note that Plato does not specify the spatial configuration that repeats after one Perfect Year. In particular, it is not restricted to conjunctions, but can be any relative arrangement of the sun, the moon, and the planets that achieves a repetition of their velocities.[5] In addition to the Perfect Number, Plato introduced the Geometric Number in a difficult passage of the *Republic* (ca. 380 BCE). It suffices to quote the following statements from this passage (*Republic* 8 546 A, D):

> Not only for plants that grow from the earth but also for animals that live upon it there is a cycle of bearing and barrenness for soul and body as often as the revolutions of their orbs come full circle, in brief courses for the short-lived and oppositely for the opposite (...) And this entire Geometric Number is determinative of this thing, of better and inferior births.

---

[4] The numbers 395 and 296 do not have a common prime factor, which is the reason why there is no shorter interval than 632 years for the repetition of the velocities of Venus and Mars. But if their periods shared a common factor, then the resulting Perfect Year would equal a fractional number of years.

[5] De Callataÿ 1996, 4 is therefore wrong in identifying the Perfect Year with a general conjunction of the planets.

The Geometric Number adds a new aspect to Plato's concept of cyclicity, namely that this property is not limited to celestial bodies, divine entities endowed with souls, but also applies to forms of life in the sublunar domain.[6] Plato includes a computation of the Geometric Number which is, perhaps by design, hard to make sense of, but it is worth pointing out that it operates with factors 3 x 4 x 5 = 60, perhaps indicative of inspiration by the Babylonian number system. The relation between the Perfect Number and the Geometric Number is not clearly specified by Plato. The following passage from the Neoplatonic philosopher Proclus (412–485 CE) may shed some light on this issue:[7]

> The number measuring the Great Year of the Timaeus is merely a part of the Geometric Number from the Republic. Whereas the Perfect Number is concerned only with the perfect return — or apokatastasis — of the eight celestial spheres of the world soul, the Geometric Number measures the return into conjunction of all spherical beings, whether belonging to the world soul (divine generation) or to the sublunar souls, which come after the gods (human generation).

According to Proclus, the Geometric Number is the period after which the universe and all beings return to their initial state. De Callataÿ adds circumstantial evidence that it was understood to be 1000 times larger than the Perfect Year, where 1000 years is the cycle for the incarnations of the soul according to Plato. Other passages in the *Republic*, e. g. the tale of the Golden Age of Kronos, and the *Timaeus*, e. g. the tale of Atlantis, provide additional details of Plato's views on the cyclicity of the world, the Four Ages, and the phases of destruction by flooding and conflagration through which the world transits in the course of one cycle.[8] No matter how the details of these doctrines may have been conceived of and, perhaps, quantified by Plato, two significant and indisputable aspects are, first, the notion that human life is subjected to cycles beyond the basic ones of the sun and the moon and, secondly, there is a very long period, named Geometric Number or Great Year, after which there will be a catastrophic destruction affecting parts of the world or the entire world. In the following well-known passage, the doctrine of a periodic destruction is put into the mouth of an Egyptian priest in conversation with the Greek sage Solon (*Timaeus* 22b–23b):

> There have been and there will be many and diverse destructions of mankind, of which the greatest are by fire and water, and lesser ones by countless other means. For in truth the story that is told in your country as well as ours, how once upon a time Phaethon, son of

---

6 De Callataÿ 1996, 10–15.
7 De Callataÿ 1996, 12–15, 108–116.
8 De Callataÿ 1996, 15–32.

Helios, yoked his father's chariot, and, because he was unable to drive it along the course taken by his father, burnt up all that was upon the earth and himself perished by a thunderbolt, — that story, as it is told, has the fashion if a legend, but the truth of it lies in the occurrence of a shifting of the bodies in the heavens which move round the Earth and a destruction of the things on the earth by fierce fire, which recurs at long intervals. (...) And when, after the usual interval of years, like a plague, the flood from heaven comes sweeping down afresh upon your people, it leaves none of you but the unlettered and uncultured, so that you become young as ever, with no knowledge of all that happened in old times in this land or in your own. Certainly the genealogies which you related just now, Solon, concerning the people of your country, are little better than children's tales; for in the first place, you remember but one deluge, though many had occurred previously; and next, you are ignorant of the fact that the noblest and most perfect race amongst men were born in the land where you now dwell, and from them both you yourself are sprung and the whole of your existing city, out of some little seed that chanced to be left over; but this has escaped your notice because for many generations the survivors died with no power to express themselves in writing.

Plato projects the image of Egypt as a deeply ancient culture in which generations of scholars had accumulated written records of the cyclical regularities underlying the catastrophic destructions of the world and of the celestial motions that cause them.[9] Even though the tale is situated in Egypt, and the motive of destructive floodings is attested across the ancient world, some elements, in particular the reference to written records that survived a flood and periodic recurrence of floods, point to the mentioned developments in Babylonia during the first millennium BCE. However, some significant differences must also be stressed. Although the Late Babylonian doctrines include methods for predicting rain and flooding based on planetary cycles, there is no evidence that the Babylonians considered these methods or the notion of cyclicity to be applicable to the catastrophic deluge that wiped out virtually all humankind in primeval times, as reported in the Flood stories contained in *Atraḥasīs*, *Gilgameš*, and other Mesopotamian compositions. As discussed in Section 2, the traditional Mesopotamian conception of time underlying these compositions does not involve a notion of cyclicity beyond the elementary calendrical cycles (day, month, year) indicated by the sun and the moon. Plato's Perfect Year gave rise to various Greco-Roman doctrines of the Great Year which will be briefly discussed in Section 11.2.

---

9 De Callataÿ 1996, 23.

9.2 Cyclicity according to Aristotle

Our exploration of this topic continues with Aristotle (384–322 BCE). The cyclical and circular nature of the motion of the stars, the sun, the moon, and the planets around the earth is a fundamental axiom of his natural philosophy as laid out in *On the Heavens*. In *Metaphysics* XII 8, Aristotle implements this axiom in a detailed model based on homocentric spheres, which is derived from earlier models by Eudoxus and Calippus. Compared to Plato, it is more difficult to pin down Aristotle's views on the existence of cyclicity below the celestial realm.[10] In *Physics* Book IV, his central text about time, we find the following statement (*Physics* IV 12):[11]

> (...) all other things are discriminated by time, and end and begin as though conforming to a cycle; for even time itself is thought to be a circle. And this opinion again is held because time is the measure of this kind of locomotion and is itself measured by such. So that to say that the things that come into being form a circle is to say that there is a circle of time; and this is to say that it is measured by the circular movement; for apart from the measure nothing else to be measured is observed; the whole is just a plurality of measures.

According to Aristotle, some consider time itself to be cyclical, because it is most naturally measured by circular movement, certainly a reference to the sun, the moon, and the planets. But the practice of measuring time by means of cyclical phenomena does not imply that time itself is cyclical. In several scattered passages, Aristotle argues for the existence of causal connections between the celestial bodies that move along the ecliptic (sun, moon, and planets) and changes in the sublunar realm. The first passage to be quoted is *Meteorology* I 339a:[12]

> We have already laid down that there is one physical element which makes up the system of the bodies that move in a circle, and besides this four bodies owing their existence to the four principles, the motion of these latter bodies being of two kinds: either from the centre or to the centre. These four bodies are fire, air, water, earth. Fire occupies the highest place among them all, earth the lowest, and two elements correspond to these in their relation to one another, air being nearest to fire, water to earth. The whole world surrounding the earth, then, the affections of which are our subject, is made up of these bodies. This world necessarily has a certain continuity with the upper motions: consequently all its power and order is derived from them. (For the originating principle of all motion is the first cause. Besides, that element is eternal and its motion has no limit in space, but is always complete; whereas all these other bodies have separate regions which limit one another.) So

---

10 De Callataÿ 1996, 32–37; Wolkenhauer 2011, 28.
11 For a discussion of this passage see Brunotte 2009, 115–116, Wolkenhauer 2011, 28–29.
12 Translation Ross 1931.

we must treat fire and earth and the elements like them as the material causes of the events in this world (meaning by material what is subject and is affected), but must assign causality in the sense of the originating principle of motion to the influence of the eternally moving bodies.

The implication is that changes in the sublunar realm are affected by the cyclical motion of the sun and the moon, and perhaps also by that of the planets. The idea that these changes are caused by the cyclical motion of celestial bodies along the ecliptic is expressed more explicitly in *On Generation and Corruption* II 10:[13]

> Now since it has been suggested and proved that coming-to-be and passing-away happen to things continuously, and we maintain that motion is the cause of coming-to-be, it is clear that, if motion is simple, both processes cannot go on because they are contrary to one another; for nature has ordained that the same thing, as long as it remains in the same state, always produces the same result, so that either coming-to-be or passing-away will always result. The movements, however, must be more than one and contrary to one another either in the direction of their motion or in their irregularity; for contraries are the causes of contraries. It is not, therefore, the primary motion which is the cause of coming-to-be and passing-away, but the motion along the inclined circle [i.e. the ecliptic]; for in this there is both continuity and also double movement. (...) The movement of the whole is the cause of the continuity, and the inclination causes the approach and withdrawal of the moving body; for since the distance is unequal, the movement will be irregular. Therefore, if it generates by approaching and being near, this same body causes destruction by withdrawing and becoming distant, and if by frequently approaching it generates, by frequently withdrawing it destroys; for contraries are the cause of contraries, and natural passing-away and coming-to-be take place in an equal period of time. *Therefore the periods, that is the lives, of each kind of living thing have a number and are thereby distinguished; for there is an order for everything, and every life and span is measured by a period, though this is not the same for all, but some are measured by a smaller and some by a greater period; for some the measure is a year, for others a greater or a lesser period.*

The highlighted part of this passage is reminiscent of Plato's *Republic* 8 546. It leaves no doubt that Aristotle assumed the existence of cyclicity in the sublunar realm and in the forms of life that inhabit it, and that their cycles are, in some manner, determined by celestial cycles. However, the cyclicity of sublunar entities is of a different kind than that of the celestial entities (*On Generation and Corruption* II 11 338 b 6–19):[14]

---

13 Translation Forster 1955. For the conception of time underlying the quoted passage (II 10 336 a15–b15) see Brunotte 2009, 109–113; Buchheim 2010, 533–542.
14 Translation Forster 1955, 329. For a commentary see Buchheim 2010, 573–578.

> Why, then, is it that some things evidently come-to-be cyclically, for example rains and air, and if there is to be cloud, it must rain, and if it is to rain, there must also be a cloud, yet men and animals do not return upon themselves, so that the same creature comes-to-be a second time. (...) The starting-point for the discussion of this problem is this, to ask the question again whether all things alike return upon themselves, or whether some things recur numerically and others only specifically.

As explained by Buchheim,[15] Aristotle distinguishes three modes of cyclicity: first, that of the celestial bodies; second, that of periodic natural processes such as the formation of clouds and rain; thirdly, phenomena of generation and destruction that are cyclical only in form, such as living creatures.

Aristotle's extant works do not preserve any reference to a Great Year after which all heavenly bodies return to the same configuration, or some other period after which all cyclical phenomena, heavenly and sublunar, return to their initial state, analogous to Plato's Geometric Year. His statements about cycles in the sublunar realm, some of which he classifies as cyclical only in form and not in number, suggest that he would not agree with the existence of such a period. However, it has been proposed that Aristotle reported a Great Year for the recurrence of planetary phenomena in some lost work. Alleged traces of his doctrine have been identified in commentaries and treatises by later scholars such as the Stoic scholar Censorinus, who lived in the third century CE.[16] In particular, a Great Year of 12,960 years, preserved as 12,954 years in the *Hortensius* of Cicero (106–43 BCE), has been attributed to Aristotle. As pointed out by de Callataÿ,[17] this number can be decomposed as a product of planetary cycles expressed in years, namely 30 (Saturn) x 12 (Jupiter) x 2 (Mars) x 1 (Venus, Mercury) x 18 (Saros cycle). The latter period is the standard Babylonian Goal Year period for predicting eclipses and the other periods are non-standard but valid Babylonian Goal Year periods. Since Babylonian astral science had penetrated the Roman empire by the time of Cicero, it is likely that these periods ultimately derive from Babylonian sources. But they are less likely to have reached Greek scholars in the fourth century BCE, although the possibility cannot be completely excluded. Furthermore, there is no Babylonian evidence for a period of 12,960 years.

---

15 Buchheim 2010, 575.
16 See de Callataÿ 1996, 32–39; Gysembergh 2013.
17 De Callataÿ 1996, 35–36.

10 Cycles and cyclicity in Greco-Roman astronomy

For Plato, Aristotle, and other Greek scholars from the fourth and third centuries BCE, the cyclical nature of the motion of the moon, the sun, and the planets with respect to the fixed stars was a certain fact. However, even those among them who specialized in astronomy, such as Eudoxus (ca. 400–340 BCE), Aratus (ca. 310–240 BCE), and Aristarchus of Samos (ca. 310–230 BCE), had little or no quantitative knowledge of the motion of the five planets.[1] In other words, their positions were considered to be potentially predictable by these scholars, but not actually so. A possible reflection of this state of affairs is expressed by Aratus in his *Phaenomena*, a work primarily concerned with fixed stars and constellations:[2]

> But there are five other stars among them, but quite unlike them, that circulate all the way through the twelve figures of the zodiac. You cannot in this case identify where these lie by looking at other stars, for they all change their positions. The years of their orbits are long, and at long intervals are their configurations when they come from afar into conjunction. I am not at all confident in dealing with them.

It is only when Babylonian data reached the Greco-Roman world from the second century BCE onward that Greek astronomy became a predictive science. The precise manner in which this knowledge circulated through the ancient world is poorly understood, but it certainly proceeded through multiple channels across different regions, with important roles for the Greek islands on the one hand and Greco-Roman Egypt on the other hand.

10.1 Hipparchus and Claudius Ptolemy

Individual scholars known to have played a major role in the "predictive turn" of Greek astronomy are Hipparchus (ca. 190–120 BCE) and Claudius Ptolemy (ca. 100–170 CE). The contributions of the former are known only through the *Almagest*, Claudius Ptolemy's treatise on mathematical astronomy, in which he makes frequent references to Hipparchus as the source of empirical data and the-

---

[1] For an introduction to their astronomical theories see, for instance, Evans 1998.
[2] *Phaenomena* 454–460 (Kidd 1997, 107); see de Callataÿ 1996, 65.

ories concerning lunar, solar, and planetary motion.[3] One example is *Almagest* IX 3, which is concerned with planetary motion:[4]

> (...) we will first set out for each of the five planets the smallest period in which it makes an approximate return in both anomalies, as computed by Hipparchus. These [periods] have been corrected by us on the basis of the comparison of their positions (...). We find, then, that for Saturn, 57 returns in anomaly correspond to 59 solar years (as defined by us, i.e. returns to the same solstice or equinox), plus about 1 3/4 days, and to 2 revolutions plus 1;43° (...); for Jupiter, 65 returns in anomaly correspond to 71 solar years (defined as above) less about 4 9/10 days, and to 6 revolutions of the planet from a solstice back to the same solstice, less 4 5/6°.

Ptolemy's aim is to construct theories that reproduce the two "anomalies", which are variations in the velocity of the planets related to (1) their elongation from the sun, i.e. variations connected to the synodic cycle, and (2) their position in the ecliptic. The text continues in a similar fashion with the periods of Mars, Venus, and Mercury. The first period relation for each planet, e.g. Jupiter's 65 returns in anomaly in 71 solar years, corresponds to a standard Goal Year period from Babylonian astronomy (Table 3). Ptolemy states that he learned about them from Hipparchus, but there is no doubt that they ultimately originate from Babylonia.[5] Analogously to the method by which Babylonian scholars derived the longer and more accurate periods of mathematical astronomy from the shorter Goal Year periods by taking into account corrections to the latter, the corrections mentioned by Ptolemy in the quoted passage would result in much longer periods for exact returns, but he is not interested in computing these periods. Instead, he continues with a computation of the mean motion of each planet for intervals of time between 1 day and 18 years taking into account the mentioned periods and the corrections in days and degrees.

10.2 The Keskintos inscription

A remarkable ancient source of information about astronomical cycles and a Great Year is the Keskintos inscription, preserved on a marble slab from Rhodes

---

3 An additional ancient source with references to the astronomical theories of Hipparchus is Papyrus Fouad 267 A which is briefly discussed in Section 10.5.
4 Translation: Toomer 1998, 423. See also Neugebauer 1975, 151; Pedersen and Jones 2010, 269–270, 296, 473.
5 Pedersen and Jones 2010, 473.

dated to about 100 BCE.[6] The inscription provides a rare window on developments in Greek theoretical astronomy between Hipparchus and Claudius Ptolemy. About three quarters of it are preserved, though difficult to read. The preserved text consists of a table of periods of Mercury, Mars, Jupiter, and Saturn, the former almost completely destroyed. They must have been preceded by a section for Venus and, less certainly, sections for the moon and the sun.[7] The table is followed by a line of text mentioning the Babylonian division of the zodiac into 360 degrees and, secondly, an otherwise unknown division of the zodiac into 27 x 360 = 9720 units called *stigmai* ("points"). The text ends with a dedication to deities, which indicates that the inscription was produced for public display. A unique feature of the inscription is that planetary periods are quantified by the number of them that fit in what amounts to a Great Year. For each planet four distinct periods are listed and, for reasons that are not entirely clear, their products with the number ten. For the present purpose two periods are singled out: first, a period "in longitude", which is the number of revolutions around the zodiac, say L; secondly, a period "in relative position (with respect to the sun)", which is the corresponding number of synodic cycles Π.[8] By adding the two numbers one obtains L+Π, which for each planet equals 29,140 and 291,400 for the ten-fold version, respectively. As argued by Jones,[9] L and Π express how many longitudinal and synodic periods fit in L+Π years. Therefore 29,140 is the number of years that contains a whole number of periods of each planet, which amounts to a Great Year. For example, the numbers for Mars are L = 15,492 and Π = 13,648, resulting in L+Π = 29,140 years, and for Jupiter they are L = 2450 and Π = 26,690, with the same result L+Π = 29,140 years.[10] The planetary periods in the Keskintos inscription are comparably or less accurate than the Babylonian Goal Year periods and they are not attested elsewhere.[11] But what motivated the selection of the seemingly arbitrary numbers 21,940 and 219,400 that function as Great Years? As argued by Jones, the underlying number from which they most likely derive is 291,600 Egyptian years of 365 days, which corresponds to almost exactly 291,400 solar years of 365.25 days. This is strongly suggested by the fact that unlike 219,400, the number 291,600 has conspicuously pleasant numerical properties, since it equals $2^4 \times 3^4 \times 5^4$ and 30 x 9720, where 9720 is the number of *stigmai* in the zodiac. These features must have

---

[6] See Jones 2006a,b,c; Bevan, Jones and Lehoux 2019, 142–145. The Keskintos inscription is overlooked in de Callataÿ 1996.
[7] See Jones 2006a.
[8] For the period Π see also Section 5.1; it corresponds to A in Jones 2006a.
[9] Jones 2006a, 19–20.
[10] For the Jupiter periods see Bevan, Jones, and Lehoux 2019, 143–145.
[11] Jones 2006a, 26; Bevan, Jones, and Lehoux 2019, 145.

motivated, by some unknown chain of arguments, the use of this number.[12] Note that the practice of representing planetary cycles as very large numbers of years is not necessarily driven by cosmological or astrological considerations, as one might think based on the writings of Plato. It could be a tool of a computational practice similar to the concept of *yuga* in Indian astronomy.[13]

10.3 The Antikythera mechanism

The Antikythera mechanism offers another unique window on cycle-based predictive methods from the period between Hipparchus and Claudius Ptolemy.[14] It was most likely produced in the first century BCE, perhaps on the island of Rhodes.[15] It has been suggested that the maker is someone close to Posidonius (ca. 135–50 BCE), an astronomer, defender of astrology,[16] and Stoic philosopher from Apamea in Syria, who lived on Rhodes. Cicero reports that Posidonius created an orrery, referred to as *sphaera*, with a function similar to the Antikythera mechanism:[17]

> (...) this *sphaera* that our Posidonius has made recently, each turning of which produces the same behavior for the Sun and Moon and five wandering stars that is produced in each day and night.

The extant remains consist of 82 bronze fragments preserving 30 gears, nearly all of which belong to the mechanism for the moon and the sun. The entire mechanism was placed in a wooden box covered by inscribed bronze plates at the front and at the back. The inscriptions on the front plate deal with planetary motion, which suggests that the mechanism included gears for the planets which are now missing. Each gear models a certain lunar, solar, or planetary period or a constitutive factor of such a period. Most of the gears for the moon are at least partly preserved. They form a highly complex mechanism that not only reproduces the mean lunar motion, but also the variations of the lunar velocity (the so-called lunar anomaly). The former gears achieve 254 revolutions of the moon around the zodiac in 19 revolutions of the sun, in accordance with a period relation

---

[12] Jones 2006a, 19–20.
[13] See Jones 2006a, 34–38; de Callataÿ 1996, 30, 132–137.
[14] See Jones 2017; Freeth et al. 2006; Freeth et al. 2021.
[15] Jones 2017, 93–94.
[16] Long 1982, 170–171.
[17] Cicero, *On the Nature of the Gods*. For a discussion of Cicero's acquaintance with Posidonius see Jones 2017, 94, 182–184, 240.

known to Babylonian and Greco-Roman scholars. The latter gears include a sophisticated co-rotating pin-in-hole mechanism that models the moon's varying velocity around the earth such that the location of highest and lowest velocity of the moon revolves around the zodiac in the opposite direction with the correct period of 8.88 years. At the back of the mechanism there are two spiraling dials. The one on the top is divided into 235 cells with month names, in accordance with the 19-year intercalation cycle. This cycle was used in Babylonia from the sixth century BCE.[18] Ancient Greek sources ascribe it to Meton of Athens (fifth century BCE), who could have discovered it independently from the Babylonian scholars. The top part also includes a secondary dial for the 76-year intercalation cycle known as the Callippic cycle. The spiral at the bottom consists of 223 cells, each corresponding to one month of the 18-year saros cycle for predicting eclipses.[19] Most cells are empty, but some of them, probably 38 out of 223, are inscribed with numbers and abbreviations to indicate an eclipse possibility in accordance with the Babylonian saros cycle. The planetary inscription on the front plate covers the planets in the Greek geocentric order Mercury, Venus, Mars, Jupiter, and Saturn. For each planet it mentions a period after which the synodic phenomena of the planet repeat at the same position in the zodiac, analogous to, but not numerically identical with, the Babylonian Goal Year periods. Based on the preserved text, the following period relations have been reconstructed for Venus and Saturn:[20]

> Venus: 289 synodic cycles = 462 years = 462 revolutions around the zodiac.
> Saturn: 427 synodic cycles = 442 years = 15 revolutions around the zodiac.

It can be assumed that these are the relations on which the missing planetary gears were based.[21] As the reader can verify, the periods differ from the known Babylonian values (Section 4.1: Tab. 3, Section 5.1: Tab. 4). They are also not attested in the Greco-Roman sources, but the terminology of the planetary inscription points to a connection with spherical models typical of Greco-Roman theory, which suggests that the periods originate from the same context. Nevertheless, it cannot be completely excluded that they originate from unknown Babylonian sources.

---

[18] Ossendrijver 2018a, 138–151.
[19] Freeth et al. 2008; Jones 2017.
[20] See Anastasiou et al. 2016, 291, 294.
[21] For a recent attempt to reconstruct the planetary gears see Freeth et al. 2021.

10.4 The *Introduction to the Phaenomena* by Geminus

The *Introduction to the Phaenomena* by Geminus (first century BCE) is an introductory treatise on spherical astronomy roughly contemporaneous with the Antikythera mechanism. The astronomical knowledge presented by Geminus has about the same elementary level as that underlying the mechanism.[22] Geminus provides a detailed account of the lunar and the solar motion in the framework of spherical astronomy. In Chapter VIII he discusses lunar and luni-solar cycles, in particular the synodic month, the 8-year intercalation cycle known as *Octaeteris*, the 19-year intercalation cycle, which he ascribes to "astronomers around Euctemon [ca. 430 BCE], Philippus, and Calippus [ca. 370–300 BCE]", and the 76-year intercalation cycle, which he attributes to Calippus. This body of knowledge of luni-solar motion is consistent with the luni-solar gears of the Antikythera mechanism. But with regard to the planets, Geminus is conspicuously silent, apart from the following statement in Book I: "We shall explain elsewhere the cause [of the variable motion] in the case of the remaining stars [i.e. the planets]".[23] However, no such work by Geminus is extant. It is therefore impossible to know the extent to which his planetary theories might have overlapped with the Antikythera mechanism. It is worth pointing out that Geminus' treatment of the lunar motion includes a description of a zigzag sequence for the moon's daily motion along the ecliptic in degrees per day based on exactly the same parameters as the corresponding Babylonian algorithm.[24]

10.5 The Oxyrhynchus papyri and the Fouad Papyrus

Other important Greco-Roman sources for knowledge of astronomical cycles beyond Ptolemy's *Almagest* are the Greek papyri from the Egyptian site Oxyrhynchus.[25] Many of the astronomical computations on the Oxyrhynchus papyri are based on Babylonian-style arithmetical methods, including lunar and planetary algorithms attested identically on Babylonian tablets. Astronomical computations based on Greek methods are primarily found on papyri written after the late third century CE. The Papyrus Fouad 267 A contains what appear to be lecture notes, most likely written in 130–300 CE, on how to calculate the motion of the sun

---

22 Jones 2017.
23 Geminus, *Introduction to the Phaenomena* Book I (Evans and Berggren 2006).
24 Geminus Introduction to the Phaenomena Ch. 18 (Evans and Berggren 2006, 99–100, 228–229); see also Jones 2001.
25 See Jones 1999.

for astrological purposes.²⁶ They make mention of three year lengths and their derivation from data ascribed to Hipparchus, a theory of solar motion different from that of Claudius Ptolemy, a period of 37,500 Egyptian years during which the sun is assumed to completes 37,473 1/3 revolutions around the zodiac, and periods of 7000 and 30,000 Egyptian years.

The Greco-Roman astronomical sources that were discussed in this chapter contain detailed knowledge of luni-solar and planetary cycles, culminating in the *Almagest* of Claudius Ptolemy. Rhodes and Egypt played important roles in the development and the dissemination of this knowledge. The saros cycle which is applied in the Antikythera mechanism and the planetary cycles used by Hipparchus definitely originate from Babylonia. Except for the Keskintos inscription and the Fouad Papyrus, the astronomical sources contain no evidence of a Great Year or other cycles of great length. But as we shall see in the next section, the existence of a Great Year was assumed by numerous Greco-Roman astrologers and Stoic philosophers.

---

26 Fournet and Tihon 2014; Tihon and Fournet 2016; Jones 2016.

11 Astronomical cycles and the Great Year in Greco-Roman astrology

In this section we explore a selection of sources in order to identify conceptions of cyclicity and their usage in Greco-Roman astrology and philosophical scholarship. The rich textual material on these topics was written by two partly overlapping groups of scholars: first, astrologers and scholars writing about astrology; secondly, natural philosophers. Their writings reflect the popularity of zodiacal astrology in the Greco-Roman world, which is the outcome of a complex process of dissemination and transformation of knowledge and artefacts between Babylonia, Greco-Roman Egypt, and the regions of the eastern Mediterranean. A common feature of the new astrological practices and doctrines is their use of the zodiac as a frame of reference for drawing inferences about events on earth from the positions of the moon, the sun, and the five planets in relation to the zodiacal signs and their subdivisions.

11.1 Horoscopy and its possible implications for the cyclicity of human fate

A most influential practice of Greco-Roman zodiacal astrology is horoscopy, also referred to as natal astrology. From Babylonia, horoscopy spread to Greco-Roman Egypt and beyond after the second century BCE. Greco-Roman horoscopes differ from the Babylonian ones in that they also report the ascendant—the zodiacal position that was rising during birth or conception. With the introduction of the ascendant, which happened in Greco-Roman Egypt, the exact time of birth or conception became an important factor for determining the fate of the newborn.

Horoscopic astrology implies the existence of connections of some sort between the positions of the moon, the sun, and the five planets and events on earth. Some Greco-Roman scholars, in particular astrologers and natural philosophers of Stoic or Aristotelian conviction, formulated theories about the nature of these connections. For Stoic philosophers the universe is a living and rational deity that controls all motion through chains of causal action extending from the fixed stars, the sun, the moon, and the planets down to the creatures on earth.¹ Manilius (first century CE) expressed this as follows in his Latin poem *Astronomica:*²

> For I shall sing of God, silent-minded monarch of nature, who, permeating sky and land and sea, controls with uniform compact the mighty structure; how the entire universe is alive in the mutual concord of its elements and is driven by the pulse of reason, since a single spirit dwells in all its parts and, speeding through all things, nourishes the world and shapes it like a living creature. (...) This God and all-controlling reason, then, derives earthly beings from the signs of heaven; though the stars are remote at a far distance, he compels recognition of their influences, in that they give to the peoples of the world their lives and destinies and to each man his own character. (...)
>
> Set free your minds, o mortals, banish your cares, and rid your lives of all this vain complaint! Fate rules the world, all things stand fixed by its immutable laws, and the long ages are assigned a predestined course of events. At birth our death is sealed, and our end is consequent upon our beginning. Fate is the source of riches and kingdoms and the more frequent poverty; by fate are men at birth given their skills and characters, their merits and defects, their losses and gains. None can renounce what is bestowed or possess what is denied; no man by prayer may seize fortune if it demur, or escape if it draw nigh: each one must bear his appointed lot.

Manilius adhered to a strict version of the Stoic doctrine of an immutable fate produced in the heavens.³ In the *Tetrabiblos*, Claudius Ptolemy applies concepts and theories borrowed from Aristotelian physics in an attempt to systematize and reformulate existing astrological doctrines and arrange them into a coherent and rational system, analogous to what he did in the *Almagest* for mathematical astronomy. Neither the *Astronomica* nor the *Tetrabiblos* were of much use for those aiming to learn astrological practice. Moreover, it would be a mistake to conclude from such treatises that all Greco-Roman astrologers were concerned with the philosophical underpinnings of their art. It seems more plausible that most of them had only limited skills and interest in dealing with such issues, which were taken up only by philosophically trained scholars.⁴

Like their Babylonian counterparts, most Greco-Roman horoscopes report the positions of the moon, the sun, and the five planets, to which is added the position of the ascendant, sometimes also that of the other three cardines (descendant,

---

1 For an attempt to identify a principle similar to the Stoic concept of *logos* in Mesopotamian cosmology see Lawson 2001.
2 *Astronomica* II 63–66, 82–87, IV 15–22. Translation: Goold 1992.
3 See Volk 2009.
4 Two Greek authors who wrote astrological handbooks with a more practical focus and relatively little attention to philosophical and theoretical aspects are Vettius Valens (second century CE) and Hephaestio of Thebes (late fourth and fifth centuries CE).

midheaven, lower midheaven). Also recall that all positions reported in horoscopes result from computation and are therefore necessarily cyclical. Some Greco-Roman astrologers concluded that inferences drawn from identical horoscopes pertaining to different dates should, in principle, be identical. Scholars skeptical of astrology turned this claim into an argument against astrology.[5] For instance, Cicero writes in *On Divination* II 97:

> Did all the Romans who fell at Cannae have the same horoscope? Yet all had one and the same end. Were all the men eminent for intellect and genius born under the same star? Was there ever a day when countless (humans) were not born? And yet there never was another Homer. Again: if it matters under what aspect of the sky or combination of the stars every animate being is born, then necessarily the same conditions must affect inanimate beings also: can any statement be more ridiculous than that?

Cicero's skepticism on the recurrence of human fate is also reflected in the following passage from *On the Ends of Good and Evil*, a Socratic dialogue about Epicurean, Stoic, and Platonic philosophy (Book II 31):[6]

> What business has a philosopher, and especially a natural philosopher, which Epicurus claims to be, to think that any day can be anybody's birthday? Why, can the identical day that has once occurred recur again and again? Assuredly it is impossible. Or can a similar day recur? This too is impossible, except after an interval of many thousands of years, when all the heavenly bodies simultaneously achieve their return to the point from which they started. It follows that there is no such thing as anybody's birthday.

Cicero denies the annual recurrence of birthdays, but he remains open to the idea of a recurrence when the planets return to the same position after thousands of years. In Book I of the *Tetrabiblos*, Claudius Ptolemy expresses the following opinion about this topic:[7]

> (...) it is furthermore true that the ancient configurations of the planets, upon the basis of which we attach to similar aspects of our own day the effects observed by the ancients in theirs, can be more or less similar to the modern aspects, and that, too, at long intervals, but not identical, since the exact return of all the heavenly bodies and the earth to the same positions, unless one holds vain opinions of his ability to comprehend and know the incomprehensible, either takes place not at all or at least not in the period of time that falls within the experience of man; so that for this reason predictions sometimes fail, because of the disparity of the examples on which they are based.

---

5 For accounts of the ancient arguments against astrology see the useful but outdated Long 1982 and the more balanced assessment by Lehoux 2012, 159–175.
6 Translation: Rackham 1931. See also de Callataÿ 1996, 44–45.
7 *Tetrabiblos* I 2 (Robbins 1980, 15–17; de Callataÿ 1996, 79–80).

Ptolemy considers it impossible to compute an exact return of all planets, most likely because this requires extremely accurate knowledge of periods and positions which cannot be obtained. The statement is consistent with his reservations about the exactness of astrology as a predictive science in comparison with that of mathematical astronomy, which he expresses at the very beginning of the *Tetrabiblos*. In *Against the Astrologers*, the Pyrrhonian Sceptic philosopher Sextus Empiricus (ca. 200 CE) argues that in order to confirm the claim that human fate repeats cyclically whenever the astronomical configuration at birth is repeated, observations of an impossibly long duration would be required.[8] He does not rule out that human fate is cyclical, but he asserts that we cannot know this. On the other hand, he does mention a Great Year of 9977 years after which the planets are supposed to return to the same positions.

11.2 The Great Year and the periodic destruction of the universe

Numerous Greco-Roman scholars present versions of a doctrine about the periodic destruction of the world, mediated by the cyclical motion of the planets.[9] The doctrine was popular among Stoic scholars from the first century BCE onward, but absent from earlier Stoic writings. The Stoic scholar Seneca (4 BCE – 65 CE) mentions it in the *Natural Questions*:[10]

> Berossus, the interpreter of Belus, affirms that these (catastrophes) occur with the movement of the planets. So positive is he that he assigns a definite date both for the conflagration and the deluge. For earthly things will burn, he contends, when all the planets, which now move in different orbits, assemble in Cancer, so arranged in one row that a straight line may pass through the spheres of all. The deluge will occur when the same gathering takes place in Capricorn. Under the former sign the summer solstice occurs, under the latter the winter solstice. These are signs with great power, as they are turning points in the very change of the year.

Seneca attributes the doctrine to Berossus, a Babylonian priest who lived in Babylon in the third century BCE. He is known as the author of the *Babyloniaka*, a Greek treatise about Babylonian culture of which only fragments are preserved

---

[8] *Against the Astrologers* Book V 103–105 (translation: Bett 2018, 217–218). See also de Callataÿ 1996, 86–87.
[9] For a comprehensive account see de Callataÿ 1996, 59–127.
[10] Seneca, *Natural Questions* 3 29 1 = Fragment F21 in de Breucker 2010; see also de Callataÿ 1996, 66–67.

through quotations in later works.[11] Seneca asserts that Berossus was able to compute the date when the planets are aligned in Cancer, which signifies a conflagration, and in Capricorn, which signifies a catastrophic flood. Several aspects of this passage require clarification. It is one of twelve extant "astronomical fragments" of Berossus, but their authenticity is contested in modern scholarship.[12] First, because the astronomical theories mentioned in them are not attested in Babylonian sources. Secondly, their content and the underlying reasoning are at odds with Babylonian methods and more in line with ideas and arguments known from Greek astronomy, which points to a Greek authorship of these fragments. But others argue that some of the fragments could belong to the *Babyloniaka* and preserve theories that were received and/or developed by Berossus through his familiarity with Greek scholarship.[13] Modern scholars agree about the fact that a doctrine of periodic catastrophes is not attested in cuneiform sources.[14] Such a doctrine would appear to contradict the traditional Mesopotamian account of the origin of the world and the course of history, as reported in mythological texts.

The Late Babylonian sources discussed above modify this picture to some extent, because they contain a wealth of cycle-based methods for predicting celestial and terrestrial phenomena. Late Babylonian scholars came to accept a much greater role for cyclicity of the world's phenomena than was assumed by earlier Mesopotamian scholars. The conceptual distance between Late Babylonian astral science and the doctrine of periodic destruction ascribed to Berossus is therefore somewhat smaller than previously thought, but it cannot be closed. Babylonian scholars developed methods for predicting rain and flooding based on planetary cycles, with an important role for conjunctions of two planets, but multiple conjunctions play no role in the extant sources. Some Babylonian astrological sources mention very long, potentially intrinsic cycles for the recurrence of flooding, reminiscent of the Great Year, but it is unclear how these periods were computed and understood. Moreover, there is no Babylonian evidence for a period after which the spatial arrangement of all planets repeats itself.

In spite of Seneca's attribution of the doctrine of periodic destruction to Berossus and a certain conceptual overlap with developments in Late Babylonian astral science, the actual roots of the Greco-Roman versions of this doctrine can be identified in the works of Plato and Aristotle. Cicero contributed to the dissemina-

---

[11] For a recent study of Berossus, the Babyloniaka, and its context see Haubold et al. 2013.
[12] Fragments F15–F22b in de Breucker 2010. See de Breucker 2013 and literature quoted therein for a skeptical position about their authenticity.
[13] Steele 2013b.
[14] Lambert 1976, 171; Brown 2018, 339–340; de Breucker 2013.

tion of Plato's doctrine through his Latin translations of the *Timaeus* and also of Aratus' *Phaenomena*.[15] The Great Year of 12,954 years which he mentions in the *Hortensius* is quoted by later authors such as Tacitus (56–120 CE) and Servius (ca. 400 CE).[16] Seneca's passage about the Great Year resonates with *Timaeus* 22b–23b, although some differences must be noted, since Plato did not specify the nature of the planetary configuration, while Seneca narrows it down to a strict alignment. The doctrine was also received and interpreted by Middle and Neo Platonic commentators.[17]

According to the Stoic astrologer Firmicus Maternus, there is "universal agreement that the *apokatastasis* (destruction) takes place through fire and flood" and this happens when the stars return to their places after a Great Year of 300,000 years.[18] There is little agreement in the ancient sources about the length of the Great Year. In fact, Firmicus Maternus reports a second value, which he refers to as the Greater Year:[19]

> Finally you (Firmicus's patron Mavortius) shifted the conversation to the *sphaera* of Archimedes and showed me the wide range of your knowledge. You described the uses of the nine spheres and the five zones, each with their different coloring. You mentioned the twelve signs of the zodiac and the effects of the five eternally wandering planets; the daily and the annual path of the Sun; the swift motion of the Moon and its waxing and waning; the number of revolutions it takes to make the Greater Year, which is often spoken about, in which the five planets and the Sun and Moon are brought back to their original places; it is completed, you said, in the 1461st year.

The "*sphaera* of Archimedes" is a reference to a device similar to the Antikythera mechanism created by the mathematician from Syracuse (third century BCE), as reported by Cicero.[20] The period of 1461 year is exemplary for many cases in which a period is taken out of its original context, in this case that of the Egyptian calendar, and recycled as a Great Year. It is known as the Sothic cycle, the period in which, due to the wandering nature of the Egyptian calendar, the heliacal rising of Sothis (Sirius) returns to Day 1 of the Egyptian year. It is of interest to note that Firmicus Maternus uses the Stoic concept of the Great(er) Year for the period in which the device produces a return of all planets to their initial positions. Even

---

15 Dowson 2023.
16 De Callataÿ 1996, 51–58; Gysembergh 2013.
17 See de Callataÿ 1996, 101–116.
18 *Mathesis* III 16 (Bram 1975, 74; de Callataÿ 1996, 75).
19 *Mathesis* I 5 (Bram 1975, 11–12; de Callataÿ 1996, 74).
20 For a discussion of Cicero's references to the mechanism created by Archimedes see Jones 2017, 130–131, 182–184.

though Firmicus Maternus does not refer to periodic destruction in the passage, it follows that he reflected on the astrological implications of such devices. The Roman grammarian Censorinus (third century CE) lists several Great Years in his Latin treatise *On the Day of Nativity* (*De die natali*), each ascribed to a different scholar. For a comprehensive list of Great Years reported by ancient and Late Antique scholars see de Callataÿ.[21] To this list one can add those inferred from the Keskintos inscription, i.e. 29,140 and 291,400 Egyptian years or 29,160 and 291,600 solar years, and the solar periods of 7000, 30,000, and 37,500 Egyptian years mentioned in the Fouad Papyrus.[22] Many of the values are vaguely resonant with Babylonian numbers, in the sense that they amount to pleasantly simple expressions in sexagesimal place-value notation. But this is insufficient ground for inferring a Babylonian origin, because sexagesimal computation had belonged to the standard toolbox of Greco-Roman astronomers since Hipparchus. A final example of a Great Year to be mentioned here occurs in the Greek treatise *On the Months* (*De mensibus*) by the Byzantine scholar John Lydus (fifth/sixth century CE):[23]

> Saturn completes its return to the same point after 265 years, Jupiter after 427 years, Mars after 284 [corrected from 294] years, the Sun after 1461 years, Venus after 1151 years, Mercury after 480 years, the Moon after 25 years. The universal return takes place after 1,753,200 years, and this is when the conjunction of all planets takes place at Cancer 30° or at Leo 1°. A deluge should occur in Cancer and a conflagration in Leo. Yet this would not be universal, as the Stoics believe it, but wholly partial.

As pointed out by Otto Neugebauer and others,[24] most of these periods coincide with values known from Babylonian mathematical astronomy (Section 5.1: Tab. 4). The only exceptions are the solar period of 1461 years, which is the Sothic period, and the lunar period of 25 years. This remarkable level of agreement implies that planetary periods from Babylonian mathematical astronomy were known by Greco-Roman astrologers and used for computing a Great Year. However, the value of 1,753,200 years does not actually correspond to the product of the individual periods, but to 1200 Sothic periods.[25] Whereas Seneca assigned the conflagration to Cancer and the deluge to Capricorn, John Lydus assigns the deluge to Cancer and the conflagration to Leo.

---

21 De Callataÿ 1996, 253–258.
22 Fournet and Tihon 2014; Tihon and Fournet 2016; Jones 2016.
23 Quoted in de Callataÿ 1996, 77–78. A similar passage with essentially the same periods occurs in a treatise by Rhetorius (sixth/seventh century CE); see Olivieri 1898, 163: lines 15–32.
24 Neugebauer 1975, 605; de Callataÿ 1996, 77–78.
25 De Callataÿ 1996, 77.

11.3 Planetary Time-Lords and their rulership over human fate

Another astrological doctrine rooted in a belief in connections between planetary periods and human fate is that of the time-lords or *chronocratores*, which is attested in Greco-Roman astrological handbooks such as Ptolemy's *Tetrabiblos*, the *Anthology* by Vettius Valens (second century CE), the *Mathesis* by Firmicus Maternus (fourth century CE), and the *Apotelesmatika* by Hephaistio of Thebes (late fourth and fifth centuries CE). According to this doctrine, the lifespan of a newborn is divided into periods of 129 months, each assigned to a planet in an order determined by their zodiacal positions at birth.[26] Some ancient astrologers refer to this doctrine as "distributions." Hephaistio of Thebes attributes it to Egypt, which is confirmed by papyrological evidence from the second century CE. No precursors of the doctrine have been identified in the extant Babylonian sources. At the end of Book IV of the *Tetrabiblos*, where Claudius Ptolemy discusses natal astrology, he introduces the doctrine as follows:

> For in the matter of the age divisions of mankind in general there is one and the same approach, which for likeness and comparison depends upon the order of the seven planets; it begins with the first age of man and with the first sphere from us, that is, the moon's, and ends with the last of the ages and the outermost of the planetary spheres, which is called that of Saturn.

The text continues with a general division of the lifespan of humans into periods assigned to the moon (4 years), Mercury (10 years), Venus (8 years), the sun (19 years), Mars (15 years), Jupiter (12 years), and Saturn (the remaining years). In other astrological treatises they are collectively referred to as "smallest" periods.[27] However, the period of Saturn is usually given as 30 years. Most of them are identifiable as astronomically correct periods known from Babylonian Goal Year astronomy, while the period assigned to the sun is known as a luni-solar intercalation cycle. Along with the "smallest" periods, some Greo-Roman astrological treatises specify "complete" and "mean" periods. All of them were used for calculating the lifespan and dividing it into distinct periods, which could be associated with time-lords. Some sources, including a newly identified papyrus from Greco-

---

26 See Zellmann-Rohrer 2023. The medieval and modern general term for astrological methods by which a lifespan is divided into periods controlled by a sequence of planets starting with the zodiacal sign of the ascendant is *profections* (Brennan 2017: 536). I thank Levente László for pointing out these doctrines.
27 Neugebauer 1975, 606.

11.3 Planetary Time-Lords and their rulership over human fate — 87

Roman Egypt[28] and the *Mathesis* by Firmicus Maternus[29], provide further details of the doctrine of the time-lords, in particular a division of each 129-month interval into periods ruled by the planets in the order which they assume at birth, such that the duration of each period expressed in months equals the number of years of the periods mentioned above, e.g. 30 months for Saturn. These brief remarks about the doctrine of the time-lords suffice to draw attention to the diverse ways in which planetary cycles were used by astrologers from at least the second century CE onward.[30] By creating a temporal framework for the lifespan of humans and its divisions, they extended the scope of their predictive methods to the length of life and the fate of the newborn in each of its phases.

---

[28] See Zellmann-Rohrer 2023.
[29] See Bram 1975.
[30] An earlier date is proposed by Tolsa 2023, 93–121, who attributes a form of this doctrine to the astrologer Critodemus (late second / early first century BCE?).

12 Concluding remarks

Our exploration of Mesopotamian and Greco-Roman scholarly sources has brought to light a rich and diverse body of evidence for conceptions of cyclicity and their applications in various contexts. The initial motivation for this study grew out of an awareness that previous research on Mesopotamian conceptions of cyclicity was mainly focused on mythological and religious compositions from the second and early first millennia BCE and has not fully engaged with Babylonian astronomical and astrological sources from the first millennium BCE. There are legitimate reasons for this. Some Late Babylonian astronomical and astrological sources have been edited only in recent times. The Babylonian astronomical diaries and related texts and the corpus of mathematical astronomy have been accessible in translation for decades, but their content is technically challenging. Another factor is that research is often scattered in disparate publications that can be difficult to keep track of, even for Assyriologists. For these reasons, a comprehensive exploration of the Babylonian sources was undertaken first in order to create a sound evidential basis for a new account of how knowledge of cyclicity, its conceptualization, and its use in predictive practices developed in Mesopotamia between the late second millennium BCE and the last centuries BCE (Chapters 2–8). In subsequent chapters (9–11) this account served as a starting point and a source of inspiration for re-examining conceptions of cyclicity in Greco-Roman scholarly sources.

The exploration of the ancient sources and the secondary literature revealed two specific aspects of temporal cyclicity that have not received sufficient attention in previous scholarship. First, the topic of planetary cycles and their importance for human existence. While notions of cyclicity imparted by the sun and the moon feature prominently in the sources that were in the focus of previous research, the role of planetary cycles, which take center stage in the Late Babylonian sources, has not received much attention in research on conceptions of time. A second aspect that has not been dealt with in a comprehensive manner concerns the cyclicity of non-astronomical phenomena, such as weather, market rates, historical events, and the universe as a whole. Are they also governed by cycles and, if so, what role is played by planetary cycles? Here too, Late Babylonian sources offer the best hope of uncovering evidence for Mesopotamian answers to these questions.

The exploratory part of this study has resulted in a better understanding of the knowledge and the conceptualization of cyclicity across Mesopotamian textual genres, periods, and regions. Several developments were pointed out. The synodic cycle of the planets emerged as an explicit concept and a central component of predictive methods in Babylonian astronomical texts after about 600 BCE. Earlier compositions, such as the astral compendium *Mul.Apin*, and the celestial omen series *Enūma Anu Enlil*, only mention constitutive intervals of the synodic cycle with no indication that they are used for predicting planetary phenomena. It is only after the "predictive turn" marked by the introduction of the Goal Year method around 600 BCE that planetary cycles were quantified and incorporated in predictive rules. The Goal Year periods contain multiple synodic cycles in order to achieve a close return in the spatial and temporal domains. They link future instances of planetary and lunar phenomena to earlier instances of the same phenomena. In other words, predictability is conceptualized in terms of periodic repetition.

The same community of scholars that produced astronomical diaries and used Goal Year methods for predicting astronomical phenomena also developed methods for predicting non-astronomical phenomena including weather, market rates, and historical events. In order to achieve this they combined two approaches to prediction. First, long-term, cycle-based prediction of planetary and lunar phenomena and, secondly, rules of the kind "if P then Q" by which non-astronomical phenomena (Q) are inferred from more or less simultaneous planetary and lunar phenomena (P). The new methodology is attested in procedure texts which explicitly state that specific categories of non-astronomical phenomena repeat after planetary Goal Year periods, thereby extending the notion of periodic repetition from the realm of planetary phenomena to the human environment.

After the introduction of the uniform zodiac near the end of the fifth century BCE, Babylonian scholars created an alternative predictive toolbox in the form of mathematical algorithms for computing essentially the same planetary and lunar phenomena that could already be predicted with Goal Year methods. With mathematical astronomy it became possible to generate tables with very long sequences of predictions, setting out from a small set of initial values. The planetary and lunar periods which are embedded in the algorithms are also longer and empirically more accurate than the Goal Year periods. It can therefore be argued that mathematical astronomy reflects a development in the mindset of the Babylonian scholars towards an even more ambitious belief in the power and the temporal scope of cycle-based prediction.

It was argued that the predictive turn in astronomy and the new methods for predicting non-astronomical phenomena reflect a major conceptual shift in the Babylonian understanding of how time is structured. Planetary, lunar, and solar phenomena were, on the one hand, assumed to be correlated with simultaneous non-astronomical phenomena along the vertical axis, more or less in accordance with the traditional view, expressed in divinatory and religious texts, that heaven and earth are interrelated. What is entirely new is the assumption of horizontal connections through time mediated by the planets. Past and future instances of planetary and lunar phenomena in heaven and on earth form repeating sequences governed by a multitude of planetary and lunar cycles, thus creating connections across long intervals of time. The resulting multi-periodic grid of temporal correspondences is superimposed on the luni-solar calendar. Explicit textual evidence for this framework is confined to relatively few scholarly texts. However, a certain awareness among the wider population of Babylonia seems plausible, because its central assumption of predictability imparted by planetary cycles was shared with astrological practices (e.g. horoscopy, medical astrology) that were used by private individuals. The Babylonian scholars developed a particular interest in planetary conjunctions, which functioned as signifying configurations for various non-astronomical phenomena. It was found that the role of the planets is often expressed in such a way that the precise nature of their agency or their role as indicators remains unclear. A striking level of agreement was noted between the hidden role of the planets in Babylonian astrology and a passage about Chaldean astral science in the *Library of History* by Diodorus Siculus.

Plato, Aristotle, Eudoxus, Aratus, and other Greek natural philosophers assumed that the planets move in cyclical orbits that were potentially predictable, but they were not actually predictable for them. Until the second century BCE, the empirical data necessary for constructing fully specified predictive models of planetary, lunar, and solar motion were not available. Greek astronomy experienced its predictive turn only after receiving Babylonian data and methods from the second century BCE onward. Subsequent astronomical sources, such as the Keskintos inscription, the Antikythera mechanism, and the Oxyrhynchus papyri, contain detailed knowledge of planetary and luni-solar cycles. The predictive turn of Greco-Roman astronomy culminated in the *Almagest*, Claudius Ptolemy's handbook of mathematical astronomy (ca. 150 CE). Some planetary and luni-solar cycles attested in the Antikythera mechanism, papyri from Greco-Roman Egypt, and the *Almagest* originate from Babylonia.

The conceptions of time and cyclicity developed by Plato have been influential in the Greco-Roman world and beyond. Some of his views on cyclicity and the role of the planets resonate with aspects of Babylonian astral science and mathematics, perhaps indicative of a certain awareness of these matters in Greek scholarly circles. For instance, Plato considered the planets to be equally important agents of time as the sun and the moon, and his definition of a planetary period corresponds to the synodic cycle, a central concept of Babylonian astronomy. Compared to Plato, Aristotle was more hesitant to assign cyclicity to non-astronomical phenomena. However, his theory of how change is possible in the sublunar realm required the cyclical motion of the sun, the moon, and the planets along the ecliptic and he admits that this can produce corresponding cyclical processes and phenomena in the sublunar realm. But Aristotle asserts that the latter forms of cyclicity are fundamentally different from the cyclicity of the heavenly motions.

With regard to the cyclicity of non-astronomical phenomena there is some minor but potentially significant overlap between Plato's views and the Babylonian doctrines. According to Plato, all life is subjected to cycles and there is a very long period of time, defined by the repetition of the velocities of all planets, after which the world is destroyed by a catastrophic fires or flooding. In the first century BCE, Stoic philosophers and Greco-Roman astrologers adopted this doctrine and they speculated about the value of the Great Year. A Great Year is also mentioned or implied in several Greco-Roman astronomical sources, such as the Keskintos inscription and the Fouad Papyrus. But apart from Seneca's questionable attribution to the Babylonian priest Berossus, no convincing trace of a Great Year or a doctrine of periodic destruction has been found in the cuneiform sources, which present the Flood as a singular historical event. There is no indication that Late Babylonian scholars changed their mind in this respect, but they did accept a much greater role for cyclicity in non-astronomical phenomena than earlier Mesopotamian scholars. It was therefore argued that the conceptual distance with the doctrine of a periodic destruction of the world is somewhat smaller than previously thought.

Along with horoscopy and other forms of zodiac-based astrology, the notion that human existence is determined by planetary cycles and human fate repeats cyclically gained popularity in the Greco-Roman world. Several examples were mentioned of doctrines in which the planets feature as rulers of certain portions of the zodiac or intervals of human life. The question of whether the cyclical nature of horoscopes implies that human fate is also cyclical was hotly debated between Greco-Roman scholars from both sides of the argument. It seems plausible that this question also came up among the Babylonian scholars who engaged with horoscopy, but no trace of a comparable discourse is preserved in the cuneiform sources.

On a final note, it is important to stress that the present investigation of conceptions of cyclicity is a limited one in terms of the ancient sources that were selected and studied. It is to be expected that a more comprehensive investigation that takes into account a broader selection of scholarly and non-scholarly sources in the Egyptian, Iranian, Aramaic, and other ancient languages would significantly enrich the results.

Bibliography

Aaboe, A. 1965. "On Period Relations in Babylonian Astronomy." *Centaurus* 10: 213–231.
Anastasiou, M., Y. Bitsakis, A. Jones, X. Moussas, A. Tselikas, and M. Zafeiropoulou. 2016. "The Front Cover Inscriptions." In *The Inscriptions of the Antikythera Mechanism*, edited by M. Allen et al., 250–297. Almagest 7.1. Turnhout: Brepols.
Angehrn, E. 1996. *Die Überwindung des Chaos: Zur Philosophie des Mythos*. Frankfurt am Main: Suhrkamp.
Assmann, J. 2011. *Steinzeit und Sternzeit. Altägyptische Zeitkonzepte*. Paderborn: Wilhelm Fink.
Bailer-Jones, D. M. 2002. "Models, Metaphors and Analogies." In *The Blackwell Guide to the Philosophy of Science*, edited by P. Machamer and M. Silberstein, 108–127. Hoboken, NJ: John Wiley & Sons.
Bailer-Jones, D. M. 2009. *Scientific Models in Philosophy of Science*. Pittsburgh: University of Pittsburgh Press.
Ben-Dov, J., and L. Doering. 2017. *The Construction of Time in Antiquity: Ritual, Art, and Identity*. New York: Cambridge University Press.
Bett, R. 2018. *Sextus Empiricus: Against Those in the Disciplines*. Oxford: Oxford University Press.
Bevan, A. Jones, and D. Lehoux. 2019. "The Miletus Parapegma and the Keskintos Astronomical Inscription." *Zeitschrift für Papyrologie und Epigraphik* 212: 137–146.
Bodnár, I. M. 2021. "The Day, the Month, and the Year: What Plato Expects from Astronomy." In *Plato's Timaeus: Proceedings of the Tenth Symposium Platonicum Pragense*, edited by C. Jorgenson, F. Karfík and Š. Špinka, 112–130. Brill's Plato Studies 5. Leiden: Brill.
Böhme, G. 1996. *Idee und Kosmos: Platons Zeitlehre – Eine Einführung in seine theoretische Philosophie*. Frankfurt am Main: Suhrkamp.
Brack-Bernsen L. 1997. *Zur Entstehung der Babylonischen Mondtheorie*. Boethius: Texte und Abhandlungen zur Geschichte der Mathematik und der Naturwissenschaften nr. 40. Stuttgart: Franz Steiner Verlag.
Brack-Bernsen, L. 2007. "The 360-day Year in Mesopotamia." In *Calendars and Years: Astronomy and Time in the Ancient Near East*, edited by J. M. Steele, 83–100. Oxford: Oxbow.
Brack-Bernsen, L., and H. Hunger. 2002. "TU 11: A Collection of Rules for the Prediction of Lunar Phases and of Month Lengths." *SCIAMVS* 3: 3–90.
Brack-Bernsen, L., and H. Hunger. 2005–06. "On the 'Atypical Astronomical Cuneiform Text E'." *Archiv für Orientforschung* 51: 96–107.
Brack-Bernsen, L., and H. Hunger. 2008. "BM 42282+42294 and the Goal Year Method." *SCIAMVS* 9: 3–23.
Brack-Bernsen, L., and J. Steele. 2004. "Babylonian Mathemagics." In: *Studies in the History of the Exact Sciences in Honour of David Pingree*, edited by C. Burnett C, J. Hogendijk, K. Plofker, and M. Yano, 95–125. Islamic Philosophy, Theology and Science, Texts and Studies 54. Brill: Leiden.
Bram, J. R. 1975. *Ancient Astrology: Theory and Practice. Matheseos Libri VIII by Firmicus Maternus*. Park Ridge, NJ: Noyes Press.
Brandes, T. 2023. *Das babylonisch-assyrische Konzept von Zeit im 2. und 1. Jahrtausend v. Chr.* Münster: Zaphon.
Brennan, C. 2017. *Hellenistic Astrology. The Study of Fate and Fortune*. Denver: Amor Fati Publications.

Britton, J. P. 2002. "Treatments of Annual Phenomena in Cuneiform Sources." In *Under One Sky: Astronomy and Mathematics in the Ancient Near East*, edited by J. M. Steele and A. Imhausen, 21–78. Alter Orient und Altes Testament 297. Münster: Ugarit-Verlag.

Britton, J. P. 2007. "Calendars, Intercalations and Year-Lengths in Mesopotamian Astronomy." In *Calendars and Years: Astronomy and Time in the Ancient Near East*, edited by J. M. Steele, 115–31. Oxford: Oxbow.

Brown, D. 2000. *Mesopotamian Planetary Astronomy-Astrology*. Cuneiform Monographs 18. Groningen: Styx Publications.

Brown, D. 2018. *The Interactions of Ancient Astral Science*. Bremen: Hempen Verlag.

Brunotte, T. 2009. "Ewige Zeit, räumliche Bewegung und göttliches Tätigsein bei Aristoteles." In *Zeit und Ewigkeit als Raum göttlichen Handelns: Religionsgeschichtliche, theologische und philosophische Perspektiven*, edited by R. G. Kratz and H. Spieckermann. Beihefte zur Zeitschrift für die alttestamentliche Wissenschaft 390, 99–122. Berlin/New York: De Gruyter.

Buchheim, T. 2010. *Aristoteles. Über Werden und Vergehen. Übersetzt und erläutert von Thomas Buchheim*. Aristoteles – Werke in deutscher Übersetzung 12. Berlin: Akademie-Verlag.

Cancik-Kirschbaum, E. 2009. "Zeit und Ewigkeit: ein Versuch zu altorientalischen Konzeptionen." In *Zeit und Ewigkeit als Raum göttlichen Handelns: Religionsgeschichtliche, theologische und philosophische Perspektiven*, edited by R. G. Kratz and H. Spieckermann, 29–51. Beihefte zur Zeitschrift für die alttestamentliche Wissenschaft 390. Berlin/New York: De Gruyter.

Civil, M. 1974. "Medical Commentaries from Nippur." *Journal of Near Eastern Studies* 33: 329–338.

Cohen, M. E. 2015. *Festivals and Calendars of the Ancient Near East*. Bethesda, MD: CDL Press.

Cwik-Rosenbach, M. 1990. "Zeitverständnis und Geschichtsschreibung in Mesopotamien." *Zeitschrift für Religions- und Geistesgeschichte* 42: 1–20.

de Breucker, G. 2010. "Beros(s)os of Babylon (680)." In *Jacoby Online. Brill's New Jacoby*, Part III, ed. I. Worthington. Accessed March 20, 2025: https://doi.org/10.1163/1873-5363_bnj_a680.

de Breucker, G. 2013. "Berossos: His Life and His Work." In *The World of Berossos*, edited by J. Haubold, G. B. Lanfranchi, R. Rollinger, and J. Steele. Classica et Orientalia 5. Wiesbaden: Harrassowitz, 15–28.

de Callataÿ, G. 1996. *Annus Platonicus: A Study of World Cycles in Greek, Latin and Arabic Sources*. Louvain-la-Neuve: Peeters.

Dowson, C. J. 2023. *Philosophia Translata: The Development of Latin Philosophical Vocabulary through Translation from Greek*. Leiden: Brill.

Emelianov, V. V., ed. 2021a. *Temporal Concepts and Perception of Time in the Ancient Orient: Proceedings of the Workshop "Calendar Festivals of the Ancient Orient" Held in St. Petersburg, 20–21 November 2020*. St. Petersburg: Eurasian Centre for Ancient Studies.

Emelianov, V. V. 2021b. "Temporal Perception in Ancient Mesopotamia." In *Temporal Concepts and Perceptions of Time in the Ancient Orient: Proceedings of the Workshop "Calendar Festivals of the Ancient Orient" Held in St. Petersburg, 20–21 November 2020*, edited by V. V. Emelianov. St. Petersburg: Eurasian Centre for Ancient Studies, 15–54.

Evans, J. 1998. *The History and Practice of Ancient Astronomy*. New York/Oxford: Oxford University Press.

Evans, J., and J. L. Berggren. 2006. *Geminos's Introduction to the Phenomena: A Translation and Study of a Hellenistic Survey of Astronomy*. Princeton: Princeton University Press.

Feliu, L. et al., eds. 2013. *Time and History in the Ancient Near East: Proceedings of the 56th Rencontre Assyriologique Internationale at Barcelona, 26–30 July 2010*. Winona Lake, IN: Eisenbrauns.

Fincke, J. C. 2015. "Additions to Already Edited Enūma Anu Enlil Tablets, Part III: a New Copy from Babylonia for the Tablet on Planets (MUL.UDU.IDIM) of the Omen Series." *KASKAL* 12: 267–279.
Forster, E. S. 1955. *Aristotle. On Sophistical Refutations. On Coming-To-Be and Passing Away.* Loeb Classical Library.
Foster, B. R. 2005. *Before the Muses: An Anthology of Akkadian Literature.* 3rd ed. Bethesda: CDL.
Fournet, J.-L., and A. Tihon. 2014. *Conformément aux observations d'Hipparque: Le Papyrus Fouad inv. 267 A.* Publications del'Institut Orientaliste de Louvain 67. Louvain-la-Neuve: Peeters.
Frahm, E. 2011. *Babylonian and Assyrian Text Commentaries: Origins of Interpretation.* Guides to the Mesopotamian Textual Record 5. Münster: Ugarit-Verlag.
Frazer, M. 2015. "Commentary on Therapeutic (šumma amēlu qablāšu ikkalāšu, bulṭu bīt Dābibi 24) (CCP 4.2.B)." *Cuneiform Commentaries Project* (E. Frahm, E. Jiménez, M. Frazer, and K. Wagensonner), 2013–2025. Accessed March 20, 2025: http://doi.org/10079/8cz8wpc.
Freeth, T. et al. 2006. "Decoding the Ancient Greek Astronomical Calculator Known as the Antikythera Mechanism." *Nature* 444: 587–591.
Freeth, T., A. Jones, J. M. Steele, and Y. Bitsakis. 2008. "Calendars with Olympiad Display and Eclipse Prediction on the Antikythera Mechanism." *Nature* 454: 614–617.
Freeth, T. et al. 2021. "A Model of the Cosmos in the ancient Greek Antikythera Mechanism." *Scientific Reports* 11, 5821. Accessed May 5, 2025: https://doi.org/10.1038/s41598-021-84310-w.
Freudenthal, H., ed. 1961. *The Concept and the Role of the Model in Mathematics and Natural and Social Sciences.* Dordrecht: D. Reidel Publishing Company.
Friberg, J. 2007. *A Remarkable Collection of Babylonian Mathematical Texts: Manuscripts in the Schøyen Collection, Cuneiform Texts I.* Sources and Studies in the History of Mathematics and Physical Sciences. New York: Springer.
Geller, M. J. 2014. *Melothesia in Babylonia. Medicine, Magic, and Astrology in the Ancient Near East.* Science, Technology, and Medicine in Ancient Cultures 2. Boston/Berlin/Munich: De Gruyter.
George, A. R. 2003. *The Babylonian Gilgamesh Epic.* Vols. I and II. Oxford University Press.
Glassner, J.-J. 2000. "Historical Times in Mesopotamia." In *Israel Constructs Its History: Deuteronomistic Historiography in Recent Research*, edited by A. de Pury, T. Römer, and J.-D. Macchi, 189–211. Sheffield: Sheffield Academic Press.
Glassner, J.-J. 2001. "Le devin historien en Mésopotamie." In *Proceedings of the XLVe Rencontre Assyriologique Internationale: Historiography in the Cuneiform World*, edited by T. Abusch et al., 181–193. Bethesda, MD: CDL Press.
Glassner, J.-J. 2004. *Mesopotamian Chronicles.* Writings from the Ancient World 19. Atlanta: Society of Biblical Literature.
Gloy, K. 1986. *Studien zur platonischen Naturphilosophie im Timaios.* Würzburg: Königshausen & Neumann.
Golinski, J. 1998. *Making Natural Knowledge: Constructivism and the History of Science.* Cambridge: Cambridge University Press.
Goold, G. P. 1992. *Manilius Astronomica.* Loeb Classical Library 469. Harvard University Press: Cambridge.
Graßhoff, G. 1999. "Normal Star Observations in Late Babylonian Astronomical Diaries." In *Ancient Astronomy and Celestial Divination*, edited by N. M. Swerdlow, 97–147. Cambridge, Massachusetts and London: MIT Press.

Gray, J. M. K., and J. M. Steele. 2008, "Studies on Babylonian Goal Year Astronomy I: a Comparison Between Planetary Data in Goal Year Texts, Almanacs and Normal Star Almanacs", *Archive for History of Exact Sciences* 62, 553–600.

Gray, J. M. K., and J. M. Steele. 2009. "Studies on Babylonian Goal Year Astronomy II: The Babylonian Calendar and Goal Year Methods of Prediction." *Archive for History of Exact Sciences* 63: 611–633.

Gysembergh, V. 2013. "Aristotle on the 'Great Year', Eudoxus, and Mesopotamian 'Goal Year' Astronomy." *Annali dell'Istituto Orientale di Napoli* 35: 111–124.

Gysembergh, V. 2023. "Babylonian Astral Sciences and Mathematics in Uruk after 47 CE." *Wiener Zeitschrift für die Kunde des Morgenlandes* 113: 69–82.

Hätinen, A. 2021. *The Moon God Sin in Neo-Assyrian and Neo-Babylonian Times.* Dubsar 20. Münster: Zaphon.

Haubold, J., G. B. Lanfranchi, R. Rollinger, and J. Steele, eds. 2013. *The World of Berossos.* Classica et Orientalia 5. Wiesbaden: Harrassowitz.

Haubold, J., J. Steele, and K. Stevens, eds. 2019. *Keeping Watch in Babylon: The Astronomical Diaries in Context.* Culture and History of the Ancient Near East 100. Leiden: Brill.

Horowitz, W. 2014. *The Three Stars Each: The Astrolabes and Related Texts.* Archiv für Orientforschung Beiheft 33. Vienna: Institut für Orientalistik der Universität Wien.

Hunger, H. 1969. "Kryptographische astrologische Omina." In *Lišān mithurti: Festschrift Wolfram Freiherr von Soden zum 19. VI. 1968 gewidmet von Schülern und Mitarbeitern*, edited by W. Röllig, M. Dietrich, K. Bergerhof, and O. Loretz, 133–145. Alter Orient und Altes Testament 1. Kevelaer/Neukirchen-Vluyn: Butzon & Bercker/Neukirchener Verlag des Erziehungsvereins.

Hunger, H. 1976a. *Spätbabylonische Texte aus Uruk I.* Ausgrabungen der Deutschen Forschungsgemeinschaft in Uruk-Warka 9. Berlin: Gebr. Mann Verlag.

Hunger, H. 1976b. "Astrologische Wettervorhersagen." *Zeitschrift für Assyriologie und Vorderasiatische Archäologie* 66: 234–260.

Hunger, H. 2001. *Astronomical Diaries and Related Texts from Babylonia V. Lunar and Planetary Texts.* Vienna: Verlag der Österreichischen Akademie der Wissenschaften.

Hunger, H. 2006. *Astronomical Diaries and Related Texts from Babylonia VI. Goal Year Texts.* Vienna: Verlag der Österreichischen Akademie der Wissenschaften.

Hunger, H. 2014. *Astronomical Diaries and Related Texts from Babylonia VII. Almanacs and Normal Star Almanacs.* Vienna: Verlag der Österreichischen Akademie der Wissenschaften.

Hunger, H. 2022. *Astronomical Diaries and Related Texts from Babylonia IV. Undated Diaries and Addenda.* Vienna: Verlag der Österreichischen Akademie der Wissenschaften.

Hunger, H., and D. Pingree. 1999. *Astral Sciences in Mesopotamia.* Leiden: Brill.

Hunger, H., and J. Steele. 2019. *The Babylonian Astronomical Compendium MUL.APIN.* London: Routledge.

Jones, A. 1999. *Astronomical Papyri from Oxyrhynchus: (P. Oxy. 4133–4300a).* Vols. I and II. Memoirs of the American Philosophical Society 233. Philadelphia: American Philosophical Society.

Jones, A. 2001. "More Astronomical Tables from Tebtunis." *Zeitschrift für Papyrologie und Epigraphik* 134: 211–220.

Jones, A. 2004. "A Study of Babylonian Observations of Planets Near Normal Stars," *Archive for History of Exact Sciences* 58: 475–536.

Jones, A. 2006a. "The Keskintos Astronomical Inscription: Text and Interpretations." *SCIAMVS* 7: 3–41.

Jones, A. 2006b. "IG XII, 1 913: An Astronomical Inscription from Hellenistic Rhodes." *Zeitschrift für Papyrologie und Epigraphik* 158: 104–110.

Jones, A. 2006c. "The Astronomical Inscription from Keskintos, Rhodes." *Mediterranean Archaeology and Archaeometry* 6: 215–222.

Jones, A. 2016. "Unruly Sun: Solar Tables and Calculations in the Papyrus P. Fouad 267 A." *Journal for the History of Astronomy* 47: 76–99.

Jones, A. 2017. *A Portable Cosmos. Revealing the Antikythera Mechanism, Scientific Wonder of the Ancient World.* Oxford: Oxford University Press.

Jones, A., and J. Steele. 2018. "Diodorus on the Chaldeans." In *The Scaffolding of Our Thoughts: Essays on Assyriology and the History of Science in Honor of Francesca Rochberg*, edited by C. J. Crisostomo, E. A. Escobar, T. Tanaka and N. Veldhuis, 333–352. Ancient Magic and Divination 13. Leiden: Brill.

Kennedy, E. S. and D. Pingree. 1971. *The Astrological History of Māshā'allāh.* Cambridge, MA: Harvard University Press.

Kidd, D. 1997. *Aratus Phaenomena. Edited with Introduction, Translation and Commentary.* Cambridge: Cambridge University Press.

Koch, U. S. 2013. "Concepts and Perception of Time in Mesopotamian Divination." In *Time and History in the Ancient Near East: Proceedings of the 56th Rencontre Assyriologique Internationale, Barcelona, July 26th-30th, 2010*, edited by L. Feliu, J. Llop, A. Millet Albà and J. Sanmartín, 127–142. University Park: Penn State University Press.

Koch, U. S. 2015. *Mesopotamian Divination Texts: Conversing with the Gods. Sources from the First Millennium BCE.* Guides to the Mesopotamian Textual Record 7. Münster: Ugarit-Verlag.

Koch, U. S. 2016. "The Meaning of Time: Mesopotamian Calendar Divination." In *Astrology in Time and Place*, edited by N. Campion and D. Greenbaum, 189–216. Newcastle upon Tyne: Cambridge Scholars Publishing.

Krul, J. 2018. *The Revival of the Anu Cult and the Nocturnal Fire Ceremony at Late Babylonian Uruk.* Leiden: Brill.

Kugler, F. X. 1907. *Sternkunde und Sterndienst in Babel: Assyriologische, astronomische und astralmythologische Untersuchungen. Vol. I: Entwicklung der babylonischen Planetenkunde von ihren Anfängen bis auf Christus.* Münster: Aschendorffsche Verlagsbuchhandlung.

Largement, R. 1957. "Contribution à l'étude des astres errants dans l'astrologie chaldéenne (1)." *Zeitschrift für Assyriologie und Vorderasiatische Archäologie* 52: 235–264.

Lambert, W. G. 1976. "Berossus and Babylonian Eschatology." *Iraq* 38.2: 171–173.

Lambert, W. G. 2013. *Babylonian Creation Myths.* Mesopotamian Civilizations 16. Winona Lake, IN: Eisenbrauns.

Lawson, J. N. 2001. "Mesopotamian Precursors to the Stoic Concept of Logos." In *Melammu Symposia II. Mythology and Mythologies. Methodological Approaches to Intercultural Influences. Proceedings of the Second Annual Symposium of the Assyrian and Babylonian Intellectual Heritage Project. Held in Paris, France, October 4–7, 1999*, edited by R. M. Whiting, 68–91. Helsinki: The Neo-Assyrian Text Corpus Project.

Lehoux, D. 2007. *Astronomy, Weather, and Calendars in the Ancient World: Parapegmata and Related Texts in Classical and Near-Eastern Societies.* Cambridge: Cambridge University Press.

Lehoux, D. 2012. *What did the Romans Know? An Inquiry into Science and Worldmaking.* Chicago: University of Chicago Press.

Livingstone, A. 1999. "The Magic of Time." In *Mesopotamian Magic: Textual, Historical and Interpretative Perspectives*, edited by T. Abusch and K. van der Toorn, 131–138. Ancient Magic and Divination 1. Groningen: Styx Publications.

Livingstone, A. 2013. *Hemerologies of Assyrian and Babylonian Scholars*. CUSAS 25. Bethesda, MD: CDL Press.

Long, A. A. 1982. "Astrology: Arguments Pro and Contra." In *Science and Speculation*, edited by J. Barnes et al., 165–192. Cambridge.

Magnani, L., and N. J. Nersessian, eds. 2002. *Model-Based Reasoning: Science, Technology, Values*. New York: Springer.

Maul, S. M. 2008. "Walking Backwards into the Future: The Conception of Time in the Ancient Near East." In *Given World and Time: Temporalities in Context*, edited by T. Miller, 15–24. Budapest/New York: CEU Press.

Mebert, J. 2010. *Die Venustafeln des Ammī-ṣaduqa und ihre Bedeutung für die astronomische Datierung der Altbabylonischen Zeit*. Archiv für Orientforschung, Beihefte 31.

Mesch, W. 2003. *Reflektierte Gegenwart: Eine Studie über Zeit und Ewigkeit bei Platon, Aristoteles, Plotin und Augustinus*. Frankfurt am Main: Suhrkamp.

Mesch, W. 2009. "Zeit und Ewigkeit in Platons Timaios: Eine Untersuchung des demiurgischen Modells." In *Zeit und Ewigkeit als Raum göttlichen Handelns: Religionsgeschichtliche, theologische und philosophische Perspektiven*, edited by R. G. Kratz and H. Spieckermann, 69–97. Beihefte zur Zeitschrift für die alttestamentliche Wissenschaft 390. Berlin/New York: De Gruyter.

Miller, K., and S. L. Symons, eds. 2020. *Down to the Hour: Short Time in the Ancient Mediterranean and Near East*. Time, Astronomy, and Calendars 8. Leiden: Brill.

Neugebauer, O. 1955. *Astronomical Cuneiform Texts: Babylonian Ephemerides of the Seleucid Period for the Motion of the Sun, the Moon, and the Planets*. London/Copenhagen/Edinburgh: Lund Humphries.

Neugebauer, O. 1975. *A History of Ancient Mathematical Astronomy*. New York/Berlin/Heidelberg: Springer.

Olivieri, A. 1898. *Catalogus Codicum Astrologorum Graecorum I. Codices Florentinos*. Brussels: Lamertin.

Ossendrijver, M. 2012. *Babylonian Mathematical Astronomy: Procedure Texts*. Berlin/New York: Springer.

Ossendrijver, M. 2015. "Babylonian Mathematical Astronomy." In *Handbook of Archaeoastronomy and Ethnoastronomy*, edited by C. L. N. Ruggles, 1863–1870. New York: Springer. Accessed March 20, 2025: https://doi.org/10.1007/978-1-4614-6141-8_192.

Ossendrijver, M. 2018a. "Babylonian Scholarship and the Calendar During the Reign of Xerxes." In *Xerxes and Babylonia: The Cuneiform Evidence*, edited by C. Waerzeggers and M. Seire, 135–163. Leuven: Peeters.

Ossendrijver, M. 2018b. "BM 32339+32407+32645 – New Evidence for Late Babylonian Astrology." In *Mesopotamian Medicine and Magic. Studies in Honor of Markham J. Geller*, edited by S. V. Panayotov and L. Vacín, 401–420. Leiden, Boston: Brill.

Ossendrijver, M. 2019. "Babylonian Market Predictions." In *Keeping Watch in Babylon: The Astronomical Diaries in Context*, edited by J. Haubold, J. Steele and K. Stevens, 53–78. Culture and History of the Ancient Near East 100. Leiden: Brill.

Ossendrijver, M. 2021a. "Weather Prediction in Babylonia." *Journal of Ancient Near Eastern History* 8: 223–258.

Ossendrijver, M. 2021b. "A Simulation-Based View on Mesopotamian Computational Practices." *Claroscuro* 20.2: 1–14.

Ossendrijver, M. 2024. "Performative Aspects of Assyrian Celestial Divination and Babylonian Astronomical Diaries." In *Manuscripts and Performances in Religions, Arts, and Sciences*, edited by A. Brita , J. Karolewski , M. Husson, L. Miolo, H. Wimmer, 39–54. Studies in Manuscript Cultures 36. Berlin: De Gruyter.

Ossendrijver, M. 2025. "Late Babylonian Reflections on the Planets as the Cause of Eclipses." In *Tempel, Tiere, Sternenhimmel. Studien zur altägyptischen Religion und Wissenschaft für Christian Leitz*, edited by F. Löffler, D. von Recklinghausen, A. Rickert, B. Ventker, 789–800. Wiesbaden: Harrassowitz.

Ossendrijver, M. and Waerzeggers, C. 2025. "Babylonian Astro-Historiography of the Late First Millennium BCE." *Zeitschrift für Assyriologie und Vorderasiatische Archäologie* 115.

Ossendrijver, M. in press. *Babylonian Mathematical Astronomy: Planetary Tables*. Cham: Springer-Nature.

Pedersen, O. and A. Jones. 2010. *A Survey of the Almagest, with Annotation and New Commentary by Alexander Jones*. New York; Dordrecht, Heidelberg and London: Springer.

Pilloni, A. 2024. "The Astrological Schemes Behind bīt niṣirtu and KI in the Babylonian Horoscopes," *Journal for Ancient Near Eastern History* 11: 1–26.

Pirngruber, R. 2013. "The Historical Sections of the Astronomical Diaries in Context: Developments in a Late Babylonian Scientific Text Corpus." *Iraq* 75: 197–209.

Rackham, H. H. 1931. *Cicero: De finibus bonorum et malorum*. Loeb Classical Library 17. London: William Heinemann.

Reiner, E. 1995. *Astral Magic in Babylonia*. Transactions of the American Philosophical Society 85.4. Philadelphia: American Philosophical Society.

Reiner, E. 2000. "Early Zodiologia and Related Matters." In *Wisdom, Gods and Literature*, edited by A. George and I. Finkel, 421–427. Winona Lake, IN: Eisenbrauns.

Reiner, E., and D. Pingree. 1975. *Babylonian Planetary Omens, Part I: Enūma Anu Enlil Tablet 63, The Venus Tablet of Ammiṣaduqa*. Bibliotheca Mesopotamica 2. Malibu: Undena Publications.

Robson, E. 2004. "Scholarly Conceptions and Quantifications of Time in Assyria and Babylonia, c. 750–250 BCE." In *Time and Temporality in the Ancient World*, edited by R. M. Rosen, 45–90. Kalamazoo: Eerdmans.

Rochberg, F. 1998. *Babylonian Horoscopes*. Transactions of the American Philosophical Society 88. Philadelphia: American Philosophical Society.

Rochberg, F. 2004. *The Heavenly Writing: Divination, Horoscopy, and Astronomy in Mesopotamian Culture*. Cambridge: Cambridge University Press.

Rochberg, F. 2010. "If P, Then Q: Form, Reasoning, and Truth in Babylonian Divination." In *Divination and Interpretation of Signs in the Ancient World*, edited by A. Annus, 19–27. Oriental Institute Seminars 6. Chicago: Oriental Institute of the University of Chicago.

Rochberg, F. 2016. *Before Nature: Cuneiform Knowledge and the History of Science*. Chicago: University of Chicago Press.

Rochberg, F. 2018. "Reasoning, Representing, and Modeling in Babylonian Astronomy." *Journal of Ancient Near Eastern History* 5: 131–147.

Rochberg, F. 2025. *Worldmaking and Cuneiform Antiquity*. Cambridge: Cambridge University Press.

Sachs, A. J., and H. Hunger. 1988. *Astronomical Diaries and Related Texts from Babylonia I*. Vienna: Verlag der Österreichischen Akademie der Wissenschaften.

Sachs, A. J., and H. Hunger. 1989. *Astronomical Diaries and Related Texts from Babylonia II*. Vienna: Verlag der Österreichischen Akademie der Wissenschaften.

Sachs, A. J., and H. Hunger. 1996. *Astronomical Diaries and Related Texts from Babylonia III*. Vienna: Verlag der Österreichischen Akademie der Wissenschaften.

Sallaberger, W. 1993. *Der kultische Kalender der Ur-III-Zeit*. Untersuchungen zur Assyriologie und Vorderasiatischen Archäologie 7. Berlin: De Gruyter.

Sallaberger, W. 2002. "Zeiteinteilung und Zeitvorstellungen im Alten Mesopotamien." In *Die Zeit im Wandel der Zeit*, edited by H.-J. Bieber, H. Ottomeyer and G. C. Tholen, 49–76. Intervalle 6. Kassel: Kassel University Press.

Schreiber, M. 2018. "Astrologische Wettervorhersagen und Kometenbeobachtungen." In *Grenzüberschreitungen: Studien zur Kulturgeschichte des Alten Orients. Festschrift für Hans Neumann zum 65. Geburtstag am 9. Mai 2018*, edited by K. Kleber, G. Neumann and S. Paulus, 739–756. Münster: Zaphon.

Schreiber, M. 2022. *Die astrologische Medizin der spätbabylonischen Zeit*. Ph.D. thesis Humboldt University Berlin. Accessed March 20, 2025: https://doi.org/10.18452/24447.

Selz, G. J. 2019. "'I Swear That These Are No Lies, It Is Indeed True!' On the Role of the Individual in Early Mesopotamian Historiography." In *Historical Consciousness and the Use of the Past in the Ancient World*, edited by J. Baines, H. van der Blom, Y. S. Chen and T. Rood, 55–68. Sheffield and Bristol: Equinox.

Singer, P. N. 2021. *Time for the Ancients: Measurement, Theory, Experience*. CHRONOI 3. Berlin: De Gruyter.

Slotsky, A. L., and R. Wallenfels. 2009. *Tallies and Trends: The Late Babylonian Commodity Price Lists*. Bethesda, MD: Capital Decisions Ltd.

Steele, J. M., ed. 2007. *Calendars and Years: Astronomy and Time in the Ancient Near East*. Vol. I. Oxford and Oakville: Oxbow Books.

Steele, J. 2011a. "Goal Year Periods and Their Use in Predicting Planetary Phenomena." In *The Empirical Dimension of Ancient Near Eastern Studies – Die empirische Dimension altorientalischer Forschungen*, edited by G. J. Selz and K. Wagensonner, 101–110. Vienna: LIT Verlag.

Steele, J. 2011b. "Making Sense of Time: Observational and Theoretical Calendars." In *The Oxford Handbook of Cuneiform Culture*, edited by K. Radner, 470–485. Oxford: Oxford University Press.

Steele, J. 2012. "Living with a Lunar Calendar in Mesopotamia and China." In *Living the Lunar Calendar*, edited by J. Ben-Dov, W. Horowitz and J. M. Steele, 373–387. Oxford: Oxford University Press.

Steele, J. 2013a. "Shadow-Length Schemes in Babylonian Astronomy." *SCIAMVS* 14: 3–39.

Steele, J. 2013b. "The 'Astronomical Fragments' of Berossos in Context." In *The World of Berossos. Proceedings of the 4th International Colloquium on "The Ancient Near East between Classical and Ancient Oriental Traditions", Hatfield College, Durham 7th–9th July 2010*, edited by J. Haubold, G. B. Lanfranchi, R. Rollinger and J. Steele, 99–113. Classica et Orientalia 5. Wiesbaden: Harrassowitz.

Steele, J. 2017. "Real and Constructed Time in Babylonian Astral Medicine." In *The Construction of Time in Antiquity: Ritual, Art, and Identity*, edited by J. Ben-Dov and L. Doering, 69–82. Cambridge: Cambridge University Press.

Steele, J. M. 2019. "The Early History of the Astronomical Diaries." In *Keeping Watch in Babylon: The Astronomical Diaries in Context*, edited by J. Haubold, J. Steele, and K. Stevens, 19–52. Culture and History of the Ancient Near East 100. Leiden: Brill.

Steele, J. M. 2020. "Short Time in Mesopotamia." In *Down to the Hour: Short Time in the Ancient Mediterranean and Near East*, edited by K. J. Miller and S. L. Symons, 90–124. Time, Astronomy, and Calendars 8. Leiden: Brill.
Steele, J. M. 2024. "Astronomical, Sequential, and Festive Time in the Late Babylonian New Year Festival." In *The Temporality of Festivals: Approaches to Festive Time in Ancient Babylon, Greece, Rome, and Medieval China*, edited by A. Walter, 11–26. CHRONOI 10. Berlin: De Gruyter.
Stern, S. 2012. *Calendars in Antiquity: Empires, States, and Societies*. Oxford: Oxford University Press.
Swerdlow, N. M. 1998. *The Babylonian Theory of the Planets*. Princeton, NJ: Princeton University Press.
Tihon, A., and J.-L. Fournet. 2016. "A New Fragment of P. Fouad inv. 267 A: The PSI inv. 2006." *Journal for the History of Astronomy* 47: 355–358.
Tolsa, C. 2023. *The Orphic Astrologer Critodemus. Fragments with Annotated Translation and Commentary*. Untersuchungen zur antiken Literatur und Geschichte 155. Berlin/Boston: De Gruyter.
Toomer, G. J. 1998. *Ptolemy's Almagest*. Princeton, NJ: Princeton University Press.
Verderame, L. 2017. "The Moon and the Power of Time Reckoning in Ancient Mesopotamia." In *The Construction of Time in Antiquity*, edited by J. Ben-Dov and L. Doering, 124–141. Cambridge: Cambridge University Press.
Volk, K. 2009. *Manilius and His Intellectual Background*. Oxford: Oxford University Press.
von Fritz, K. 1971. *Grundprobleme der Geschichte der antiken Wissenschaft*. Berlin/New York: De Gruyter.
von Lieven, A. 2017. "Divine Figurations of Time in Ancient Egypt." In *The Construction of Time in Antiquity: Ritual, Art, and Identity*, edited by J. Ben-Dov and L. Doering, 97–123. Cambridge: Cambridge University Press.
van der Spek, R. J., I. Finkel, R. Pirngruber, K. Stevens 2025. *Babylonian Chronographic Texts from the Hellenistic Period*. Atlanta: SBL Press.
van der Waerden, B. L. 1957. "Babylonische Planetenrechnung." *Vierteljahrsschrift der Naturforschenden Gesellschaft in Zürich* 102: 39–60.
Wee, J. 2015. "Discovery of the Zodiac Man in Cuneiform." *Journal of Cuneiform Studies* 67: 217–233.
Wilcke, C. 1988. "Die Sumerische Königsliste und erzählte Vergangenheit." In *Vergangenheit in mündlicher Überlieferung*, edited by J. von Ungern-Sternberg, 113–140. Colloquium Rauricum 1. Stuttgart: Franz Steiner Verlag.
Wilcke, C. 1999. "Weltuntergang als Anfang: Theologische, anthropologische, politisch-historische und ästhetische Ebenen der Interpretation der Sintflutgeschichte im babylonischen Atramḫasīs-Epos." In *Weltende: Beiträge zur Kultur- und Religionswissenschaft*, edited by A. Jones, 63–112. Wiesbaden: Harrassowitz.
Winsberg, E. 1999. "Sanctioning Models: The Epistemology of Simulation." *Science in Context* 12: 275–292.
Winsberg, E. 2009. "Computer Simulation and the Philosophy of Science." *Philosophy Compass* 4.5: 835–845.
Wolkenhauer, A. 2011. *Sonne und Mond, Kalender und Uhr: Studien zur Darstellung und poetischen Reflexion der Zeitordnung in der römischen Literatur*. Untersuchungen zur antiken Literatur und Geschichte 103. Berlin: De Gruyter.
Zellmann-Rohrer, M. 2023. "The Chronokratores in Greek Astrology, in Light of a New Papyrus Text: Oxford, Bodl. MS gr. class. B 24 (P) 1–2." *Harvard Studies in Classical Philology* 112: 465–502.

Index of Names

Aratus   72, 84, 90
– *Phaenomena*   72, 84
Archimedes   84
Aristarchus of Samos   72
Aristotle   69–72, 80, 83, 90 f.
– *Metaphysics*   69
– *Meteorology*   69
– *On Generation and Corruption*   70
– *On the Heavens*   69
– *Physics*   69
Artaxerxes   21 f., 40

Berossus   4, 82 f., 91
– *Babyloniaka*   4 f., 82 f.

Calippus   69, 77
Censorinus   71, 85
– *On the Day of Nativity*   85
Cicero   71, 75, 81, 83 f.
– *Hortensius*   71, 84
– *On Divination*   81
– *On the Ends of Good and Evil*   81
Claudius Ptolemy   72 f., 77 f., 86, 90
– *Almagest*   72 f., 77 f., 80, 90
– *Tetrabiblos*   80–82, 86

Darius   40
Diodorus Siculus   62 f., 90
– *Library of History*   62, 90

Euctemon   77
Eudoxus   69, 72, 90

Firmicus Maternus   84–87
– *Mathesis*   84, 86 f.

Geminus   77
– *Introduction to the Phaenomena*   77

Hephaistio of Thebes   86
– *Apotelesmatika*   86
Hipparchus   72–75, 78, 85

John Lydus   59, 85
– *On the Months*   85

Manilius   80
– *Astronomica*   80
Marduk   5 f., 14, 56
Māshā'allāh   39, 41
Meton of Athens   76

Nabû   41
Nannar   6

Philippus   77
Plato   64–72, 75, 83 f., 90 f.
– *Republic*   66 f., 70
– *Timaeus*   64 f., 67, 84
Posidonius   75
Proclus   67

Šamaš   6, 40, 54, 56
Seneca   4, 82–85, 91
– *Natural Questions*   82
Sextus Empiricus   82
– *Against the Astrologers*   82
Sîn   6, 56
Solon   67 f.

Tiamat   5

Xerxes   40

General Index

acronychal rising   16
agency   2, 6, 55–57, 61, 90
– causal agency   2, 56f., 61
– hidden agency   55f.
– planetary agency   55–58, 61, 90
Almanacs   18, 24, 26, 28–30, 49
angular distance   19f.
annual phenomena   17
anomaly   73, 75
antediluvian   4f.
Antikythera mechanism   64, 75, 77f., 84, 90
Apamea   75
ascendant   79f., 86
astrology   39, 51, 54f., 75, 79–87, 90f.
astronomical diary   14–18, 21, 24–30, 32, 35, 40–46, 60f., 88f.
Atraḫasīs   4, 68

Babylon   14, 23f., 28, 40, 43, 50, 56f., 103
Baghdad   39, 41
bala   5, 34
barley   42f., 45
benefic   25, 48f., 59
Borsippa   38
brightness   45, 48f.

calendar   1f., 6f., 10, 13f., 17, 19f., 22, 29, 39, 52–54, 84
   Babylonian calendar   16–21, 29
– Calendar Text   52–55
– Calendar Text scheme   53f.
celestial divination   16, 49, 51
celestial equator   65
Chaldeans   62f.
Chronicles   41, 50
chronocratores   86
chronology   12, 29f.
close return   11, 19–21, 30, 35, 39, 60, 89
cloud   18, 30, 43, 46f., 71
comet   17f., 30, 62
compendium   25, 38, 50, 89
composite cycle   30, 37

computation   33, 51, 59, 61, 66f., 73, 77, 81, 85
– computational toolbox   33
– retro-computation   60
conflagration   67, 82f., 85
conjunction   6, 16, 19, 37–41, 47–49, 52, 57f., 61, 66f., 72, 83, 85
– planetary conjunction   37–39, 41, 57, 61, 90
coordinate   32
– coordinate frame   32
crescent   16
cubit   15, 23, 40f.
cyclical time   1

daily   15, 23, 43, 52–55, 65f., 77, 84
– daily motion table   33, 49
– daily position   33, 49
data processing   29
Demiurge   64
descendant   80
difference   33f., 68, 84
– difference quantity   33
distributions   86
divination   1, 8–13, 40
Dodecatemoria scheme   52–54

eclipse   17, 26f., 43, 56f., 62f., 71, 76
– lunar eclipse   17, 27
– solar eclipse   17, 28, 37, 43, 56
ecliptic   15, 20, 32, 34, 37, 49, 64, 69f., 73, 77, 90
Egypt   2, 51, 68, 72, 78f., 86f., 90
– Egyptian Year   74, 78, 84f.
elongation   37, 73
emic   34
Enūma Anu Enlil   10–13, 17, 20, 30, 44f., 58, 89
Enūma eliš   4f., 7
Epicurean   81
equinox   17, 73
Esagila   14
Euphrates   15, 42f., 48

evening first   8, 11, 36
evening last   8, 11

faintness   45, 49
fate   52, 62, 79–82, 86 f, 91
finger   15, 41
first appearance   9, 11, 13, 16, 20, 24, 37, 40, 46, 48
Flood   4, 48, 61, 68, 83 f.
Fouad Papyrus   77 f., 85, 91

Geometric Number   66 f.
Gilgameš   4, 68
Goal Year   24–30, 40, 49, 58, 61, 86
– Goal Year method   14–27, 30–33, 35, 39, 41 f., 45, 48 f., 59 f., 89
– Goal Year period   18–27, 29 f., 33–35, 38 f., 45–47, 60, 71, 73 f., 76, 89
– Goal Year procedure   23–25, 38, 45, 50, 60
– Goal Year text   18, 24, 26, 28–30, 49
Great Year   5, 37, 51, 59, 61 f., 64, 67 f., 71, 73 f., 78 f., 82–85, 91

– heliacal rising   17, 84
– heliacal setting   17
heliocentric   21
historiography   1
– astrological historiography   40 f.
horoscope   51 f., 79–81, 91
– horoscopy   51 f., 79, 90 f.

inference   2 f., 47, 49, 52, 79, 81
– inferential rule   44, 47, 49, 60
– inferential statement   47, 61 f.
instruction   23 f., 30, 44, 48, 54, 62
intercalation   11, 26, 46, 76 f., 86
– intercalary month   19
– intercalary year   15, 29
interval of invisibility   8 f., 12
interval of visibility   8 f., 11–13
intrinsic   50 f., 83
– intrinsic cyclicity   50
– intrinsic period   50

Jupiter   8 f., 16, 21, 25, 27 f., 36, 39, 41, 45, 47–49, 55–58, 71, 73 f., 76, 85 f.

Keskintos inscription   64, 73 f., 78, 85, 90 f.

last appearance   9 f., 16, 19, 22, 24, 45, 49
Late Babylonian   1, 5, 14, 23–25, 30, 33, 37, 39 f., 43 f., 49 f., 54–58, 60 f., 63–65, 68, 83, 88, 91
library   15, 58
linear time   1
longitude   32–35, 53, 74
loosening of the sandal   46
Lunar Six interval   15–17, 26 f., 43
– NA_1 16 f
– luni-solar   4, 17, 61, 77 f., 86
– luni-solar calendar   5, 55, 90
– luni-solar cycle   1, 52 f., 77, 90

malefic   25, 41, 48 f., 59
market phenomena   49
market rate   15, 30, 37, 42–45, 47–50, 57, 60, 88 f.
Mars   8, 16, 21, 25, 34, 36, 38–41, 45, 48 f., 55–59, 66, 71, 73 f., 76, 85 f.
mathematical astronomy   5, 31–36, 49, 52, 57, 59–61, 66, 72 f., 80, 82, 85, 88–90
melothesia
– planetary melothesia   55 f.
– zodiacal melothesia   56
Mercury   12, 16, 25, 36, 38–41, 45, 48, 55, 57 f., 71, 73 f., 76, 85 f.
meteor   17 f.
microzodiac   52, 54 f.
midheaven   81
– lower midheaven   81
model   2 f., 26, 35, 52, 55, 69, 75 f., 90
– model-based knowledge production   61
– modeling   2
Moongod   4, 6, 55 f., 58
morning first   8, 11, 36
morning last   8, 11
Mul.Apin   9 f., 12 f., 17, 30, 89

Neo-Assyrian   30
Normal Star   15, 17 f., 21–23, 25, 28–30, 38, 45, 47, 49
– Normal-Star Almanac   18
– Normal-Star passage   15
Normal Stars   15, 25

observation   18, 28, 45, 49, 52, 62, 82
Octaeteris   77
Old Babylonian   12
omens   10–12, 37, 57–59, 61
opposition   6, 16, 19, 37, 47f., 57, 61
orbital period   19, 21
Oxyrhynchus   77, 90

Perfect Number   65–67
Perfect Year   65–68
period relation   13, 34f., 73, 75f.
personal turn   51
Pleiades   47
postdiluvian   4
predictability   30, 44, 49, 60f., 66, 89f.
prediction   10, 18, 21, 24–33, 35, 37, 44–51, 57–60, 81, 89
- long-term prediction   44f., 48–50
- predictive turn   14, 31, 60, 72, 89f.
priest   4, 67, 82, 91
procedure text   23–26, 30, 32, 34, 38, 44, 49f., 60–62, 89

recurrence rule   44, 61
regular watch   15
reign   5, 12, 34
revolution   15, 20f., 34–36, 52, 62, 65f., 73–76, 78, 84
Rhodes   73, 75, 78
river level   43

saros cycle   26, 37, 71, 76, 78
Saturn   8f., 12f., 16, 25, 36, 38–41, 45, 47f., 55, 57f., 71, 73f., 76, 85–87
schematic year   11f., 52
scholars   1f., 5, 8f., 12–16, 18, 20f., 23f., 26–28, 30, 33f., 37, 40–43, 46, 49, 52, 55, 60–62, 68, 71–73, 76, 79–83, 85, 89–91
sexagesimal place value notation   33f., 38, 57
sign entry   17
Sippar   38
solar distance principle   37

solstice   17, 73, 82
Sothis   84
- Sothic cycle   84
sphaera   75, 84
station   16f., 19, 45, 65
- first station   16
- second station   16
step function   34
Stoic   71, 75, 78–82, 84f., 91
Stone-Plant-Wood Scheme   54
sublunar   67, 69–71, 90f.
Sumerian King List   4f., 34
Sungod   6, 55f.
synodic   8f., 13, 16f., 19–25, 28, 30, 33–39, 45, 49, 52, 76f.
- synodic arc   20, 33–35
- synodic cycle   8–13, 16, 19f., 23, 30, 34–37, 60, 65f., 73f., 76, 88–90
- synodic period   19, 65f., 74
- synodic table   33, 49
system A   34
system B   34

temple   14, 23, 55f.
terrestrial phenomena   30, 49, 60f., 83
three stars each   6

velocity   37, 65, 73, 75f.
Venus   9–12, 16, 19–26, 28, 34–36, 39, 45, 48, 55, 57f., 66, 71, 73f., 76, 85f.
- *Venus tablet of Ammiṣaduqa*   12

weather phenomenon   45–47
worldmaking   2

- zigzag sequence   34, 77
zodiac   15f., 18, 20, 47, 52–54, 56, 72, 74–76, 78, 84, 91
- uniform zodiac   32, 47, 51f., 60, 89
- zodiacal position   33, 52, 54, 79, 86
- zodiacal sign   17, 32, 45, 47f., 51–54, 56f., 79, 86

The following volumes have been published in this series:

Volume 2
Detel, Wolfgang. *Subjektive und objektive Zeit: Aristoteles und die moderne Zeit-Theorie.* Berlin/Boston: De Gruyter, 2021.

Volume 3
Singer, P. N. *Time for the Ancients: Measurement, Theory, Experience.* Berlin/Boston: De Gruyter, 2022.

Volume 4
Gertzen, Thomas L. *Aber die Zeit fürchtet die Pyramiden: Die Wissenschaften vom Alten Orient und die zeitliche Dimension von Kulturgeschichte.* Berlin/Boston: De Gruyter, 2022.

Volume 6
Zachhuber, Johannes. *Time and Soul: From Aristotle to St. Augustine.* Berlin/Boston: De Gruyter, 2022.

Volume 7
Golitsis, Pantelis. *Damascius' Philosophy of Time.* Berlin/Boston: De Gruyter, 2023.

Volume 8
Defaux, Olivier. *La Table des rois: Contribution à l'histoire textuelle des ›Tables faciles‹ de Ptolémée.* Berlin/Boston: De Gruyter, 2023.

Volume 9
Fischer, Julia (Hrsg.). *Zwiegespräche über die Zeit: Dialoge in der Berlin-Brandenburgischen Akademie der Wissenschaften aus Anlass des sechzigsten Geburtstags von Christoph Markschies.* Berlin/Boston: De Gruyter, 2024.

Volume 10
Walter, Anke (Hrsg.). *The Temporality of Festivals: Approaches to Festive Time in Ancient Babylon, Greece, Rome, and Medieval China.* Berlin/Boston: De Gruyter, 2024.

Volume 12
Sieroka, Norman. *Zeit-Hören: Erfahrungen, Taktungen, Musik.* Berlin/Boston: De Gruyter, 2024.

Volume 13
Birk, Ralph/Coulon, Laurent (Hrsg.). *The Thebaid in Times of Crisis: Revolt and Response in Ptolemaic Egypt.* Berlin/Boston: De Gruyter, 2025.

Volume 14
Pallavidini, Marta. *(A)synchronic (Re)actions: Crises and Their Perception in Hittite History.* Berlin/Boston: De Gruyter, 2025.

Volume 15
Nosch, Marie-Louise, Bech. *Time and Textiles in Ancient Greece.* Berlin/Boston: De Gruyter, 2025.

Volume 16
Klinger, Jörg. *Das Erfassen von Zeit im Kontext der Vergangenheit.* Berlin/Boston: De Gruyter, 2026.

Volume 17
Zachhuber, Johannes. *Time and History in Denis Pétau. Philosophy, Science, and Religion in Early Modern France.* Berlin/Boston: De Gruyter, 2026.

www.ingramcontent.com/pod-product-compliance
Lightning Source LLC
Chambersburg PA
CBHW070317240426
43661CB00057B/2673